I0420631

The Kah'Mari Desposyni

Sephardic Roots of Royal and Spanish Diaspora Of the Family lineage of Christ, Merari and Aaron

BY:
Rev. Cpt. Daniel W Merrick PhD ME

© 2015 Eternal Light & Power Company Publishing
Daniel W Merrick PhD; CYMG, Smethport, Pa. 16749
www.YahBible.com

Table of Contents

FORWARD..3
How We Are Defined..9
Merari Of Merarites..22
YDNA..25
MT DNA..30
A Prophet Is Without Honor......................................32
Terms Of Endearment..41
Merarite Clan..44
Abba Mari ben Moses..46
Barbados..46
Dating Bias..47
The Kah'Mari Desposyni..51
The Kah'Mari Desposyni from Scriptures..................60
The Merrick Connection:..61
References:..82
Bibliography..85
Conclusion..94
Last Page 96

ISBN-13: 978-1518796913

ISBN-10: 1518796915

FORWARD

When thinking of history we do not often come upon a notion that what we have been taught is not what is actual facts because we read it in a text book in school. Yet the documented facts of rewrites of history to favor a point of view has been noticed in these later years of mankind with the advent of social networks and the internet giving us all the means to publish sources and little known factual items. This opened the door for media to lose it's grasp on content and even governments from preventing the evidence of their version of the story not being factual or historically correct. I often have said that the important thing ignored by most large media outlets is not the story itself, but the spin and slant of how the story is told and the perspective of who is telling the history. Control the message and you control the knowledge with the media.

To spite many media and printing outlets attempting to stop truth from coming to light, for what ever the motives are that they do these things, is the major problem most unknown history and truth has been kept from the people via the air waves of TV and Radio until lately.

One of the best example of this fact of allowances of one to get heard on the air, and another to be black balled from gaining air time or even interviews for their books and amazing discoveries, is the case of the Smithsonian Institute doctrine and dogma of the Manifest Destiny in the early 1800s.

The official government version of the God given Manifest Destiny of the United States was that the British and Christian message had a Destiny to populate and convert the masses of heathen native American and expand the country west. Yet as early as the 1600's and 1700's the facts on the ground from archaeologists and discoveries being made was that the Heathens were not really so much in need of conversion as the doctrine taught. In fact, the real story of who came to America long ago before Columbus in 1492 was being discovered when Hebrew language artifacts were found in the Burial mounds of Ohio and in the Paleo Hebrew Ten Commandments written in stone in New Mexico. This evidence when gained into the archives of the Smithsonian became suppressed and hidden for hundreds of years because it did not match the doctrine to which they were compromised to hide the truth.

Front   Back

Hebrew Lettering found on artifacts in Mounds in Ohio

This is where we pick up our story on what happened before this great expansion into the west promoted by the president and the Christian nation to fulfill their Manifest Destiny. So lets go back to the time of Slavery in Egypt

4

and pick up the story of the Mari and Diaspora that came before the time of Christ.

These many facts and artifacts proved that a Hebrew pre-discovery of Columbus, the Catholic version of the story, and the Protestant so called "Destiny", may have been to convert what was thought the heathen, who in fact were from Hebrew tribal origins.

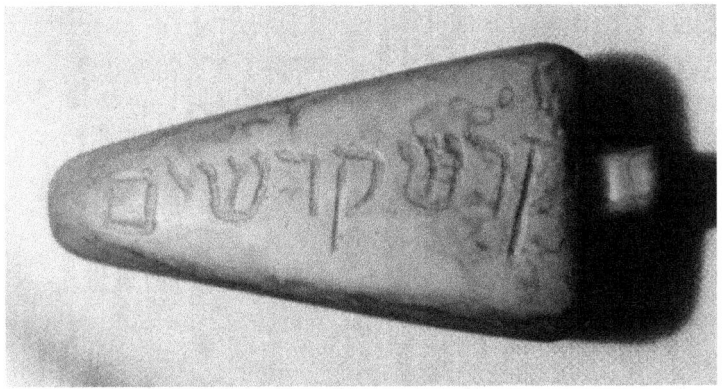

Hebrew Letters on artifact found in North America

Ten Commandments In Stone In New Mexico in Paleo Hebrew

It is widely known that reporting on everything from politics to history in education and media and even publishing books has always had a bias. This is often referred to in accounts of wars, that the victors write the history and therefore the influences of reasoning is a mirror of what the writer believes or is biased to report.

The discoveries of Paleo Hebrew, Middle Hebrew and the block lettering of even the Tetragrammaton of the name of God, YHUH, found in America proves that there was more than one migration of Hebrew people long before Columbus or even the Vikings came to America.

In my presentation in this book, I will start with the migrations known and the evidence we now have that proves these migrations, and tie them into the phonetic records that show in names and places, people and tribes, how the Hebrew people, both Orthodox and Messianic came from the seed of Jacob who was called Israel in the Tanak (Old Testament) and settled in what is now called North and South America.

In light of prophesy about the Hebrew tribes found in the bible, it might be important to note that the ties of Israel as a people is interwoven into the Americas and present day Israel as genetic offspring from the dispersions of the chosen people. The idea of AM-ISREAL as it has been called by some scholars, is not new, but is also provable by evidence and science. I am not talking about some crypto-jewish dogma or doctrines of theory in this book, but of the documented evidences of report by such documentary presentations of Hebrew lines that came to places like Barbados[1] in migrations after the 1400's CE and films like that on JLTV the J-Report[2] about *Ladino* and Sephardic Jews in South America. The studies done by Dr Davies[3] of Oxford on the Hebrew and Egyptian ties to Mummies found in Egypt dating back to as late as 1500 to 3000 BCE also gives rise to evidence that if accepted by modern academia would rewrite many history books.

The criticisms of this theory, in such papers as "American Drugs in Egyptian Mummies" by S.A. Wells citations on the subject, have in part been dispelled as old school attempts to hold on to historical accounts that do not line up with evidence in light of DNA studies done by FTDNA and papers listed which support the Cohanim Sephardic links found in recent studies of Ladino and Native American genetic samples.

Wells writes *"The recent findings of cocaine, nicotine, and hashish in Egyptian mummies by Balabanova et. al. have been criticized on grounds that: contamination of the mummies may have occurred, improper techniques may have been used, chemical decomposition may have produced the compounds in question, recent mummies of drug users were mistakenly evaluated, that no similar*

---

1 J Report Episode 43: Latin American Jews; AIR, LAND, AND SEA: THE JEWS OF BARBADOS "discover the history of one of the earliest Jewish communities in the Americas " http://jltv.tv/videos.php?id=65&play=1865

2 REF: J Report #24 - Sephardic Jews and Ladino; "Discovering Sephardic Jewry, Jews of the Iberian Peninsula and their unique language, Judeo-Spanish or Ladino. " http://www.jltv.tv/video.php?user=JReport&video_id=614

3 The mystery of the cocaine mummies; http://www.druglibrary.org/schaffer/misc/mummies.htm; http://www.faculty.ucr.edu/~legneref/ethnic/mummy.htm

cases are known of such compounds in long-dead bodies, and especially that pre-Columbian transoceanic voyages are highly speculative. "

It is this attitude with academia that seeks to protect their royalties for text books, along with the shelter of evolutionary doctrines of the cult of education that demands we all accept that there is no God, that has driven the blindness to the facts as they hold there hands over their eyes like the "see no evil" monkey that says he sees no proof.

So let us with open eyes venture into the migrations and ancestry of the Merarite Jews and the Mari of the Americas, to show how the American-Israel connection is found in history with facts and DNA scientific evidences and documentation.

How We Are Defined

The Jewish diaspora (Hebrew: Tfoot'za, תפוצה) or Exile (Hebrew: Galut, גלות; Yiddish: Golus) refers to the dispersion of Israelites, Judahites, and later Jews out of what is considered their ancestral homeland (the Land of Israel) and the communities built by them across the world.[4]

Pre-Roman diaspora

In 722 BCE, the Assyrians, under Sargon II, successor to Shalmaneser V, conquered the Kingdom of Israel, and many Israelites were deported to Mesopotamia.[5] This is found in the Bible in the book of Ezra and other places where the tribes married "Strange wives" meaning goyim or gentiles. When the time came to return for many, some were not allowed by the leadership because of inner marriages with those who were not from the tribes of Israel.

This was in particular important to some tribal lines in that the commandments of Torah required that with the Levite and Priests that they not take wives who were not from the seed of Abraham, Issac, and Jacob.

Ezra 10:10-11 And Ezra the priest stood up, and said unto them, Ye have transgressed, and have taken strange wives, to increase the trespass of Israel. Now therefore make confession unto **YHUH** *the LORD God* of your fathers, and do his pleasure: and separate yourselves from the people of the land, and from the strange wives.

---

4   https://en.wikipedia.org/wiki/Jewish_diaspora
5   Laura A Knott (1922) *Student's History of the Hebrews* p.225, Abingdon Press, New York

Then we have the Babylonian captivity and return after the divisions of Israel into two kingdoms under Solomon.

As early as the middle of the 2nd century BCE the Jewish author of the third book of the Oracula Sibyllina addressed the "chosen people," saying: "Every land is full of thee and every sea." [6]

Roman rule, which began in 63 BCE, continued until a revolt from CE 66–70, a Jewish uprising to fight for independence, was eventually crushed after four years, culminating in the capture of Jerusalem and the burning and destruction of the Temple, the centre of the national and religious life of the Jews throughout the world. Jerusalem was also destroyed.

The Jewish Diaspora at the time of the Temple's destruction, according to Josephus, was in Parthia (Persia), Babylonia (Iraq), Arabia, as well as some Jews beyond the Euphrates and in Adiabene (Kurdistan). In Josephus' own words, he had informed "the remotest Arabians" about the destruction. [7]

Many went in this era to Egypt or further south into the Arabian peninsula, while still others went into eastern Europe and Africa with some who went to join with the remnants of other dispersions into China, India, or around the world. The reports of an earlier migration came to light with the talk of Atlantis and a land across the great

---

6   The **Sibylline Oracles** (Latin: *Oracula Sibyllina*; sometimes called the "pseudo-Sibylline Oracles") are a collection of oracular utterances written in Greek hexameters ascribed to the Sibyls, prophetesses who uttered divine revelations
     https://en.wikipedia.org/wiki/Sibylline_Oracles
7   https://en.wikipedia.org/wiki/Jewish_diaspora

sea.

In Rome the Arch of Titus[8]

During the Middle Ages, due to increasing geographical dispersion and re-settlement, Jews divided into distinct regional groups which today are generally addressed according to two primary geographical groupings: the Ashkenazi of Northern and Eastern Europe, and the Sephardic Jews of Iberia (Spain and Portugal), North Africa and the Middle East. These groups have parallel histories sharing many cultural similarities as well as a series of massacres, persecutions and expulsions, such as the expulsion from Spain in 1492, the expulsion from England in 1290, and the expulsion from Arab countries in 1948–1973.[9]

From the pales of Russia to the Germany of World War II the Jews and Hebrew people have been killed, persecuted, and hated as proven by the Shoah of Auschwitz to the Persian Haymen of the book of Ester. In one old joke on

---

8   *Kleiner, Fred (2010). Gardner's Art Through the Ages: A Global History, Enhanced, Volume I: 1. Wadsworth Publishing. p. 262. ISBN 1439085781.*

9   https://en.wikipedia.org/wiki/Jewish_ethnic_divisions

this topic an old Rabbi is standing at a check point with his papers and passport being checked by the broader guard as he is processed out of the country from which he is being expelled. The caption on the cartoon has the Rabbi saying *"I have been thrown out of better countries than this one"*.

As if the Holocaust was not enough, we have Tevye in *Fiddler on the Roof* saying as he is thrown out of Russia in a prayerful joke with Ha Shem, *"Could you choose someone else for a change".* [10]

But in all this history and every account we are left with a gap and some controversy. The first being that of the Genetic origins of who is really a Jew or an Israelite. Modern Jewish remnants of what remain of the Hebrew people in the world became scared and timid throughout the ages with each new persecution. Fear set in and the tools used to mark for death those of us who were "Jude" or *"Yahudie"* became the very thing these survivors resisted in finding family in dispersion in the nations of the world. The thought of a "Jewish Gene" of DNA that could mark us as a people, tribes, and original Hebrew, many feared in it's so called scientific use to exterminate us in the lands we sought refuge in.

Nazi scientists so called, claimed to find out by eye color, nose size, shape of the head, hair color, and other obscure reasons who was a Jew and use it to exterminate million in gas chambers and such designs of Eugenics for mass murder.

---

10 **Tevye the Dairyman** ([ˈtɛvjə], Yiddish: טביה דער מילכיקער) adapted story from the 1939 film later in 1964 remade into a musical. *Fiddler on the Roof* is based on *Tevye and his Daughters* ; https://en.wikipedia.org/wiki/Tevye

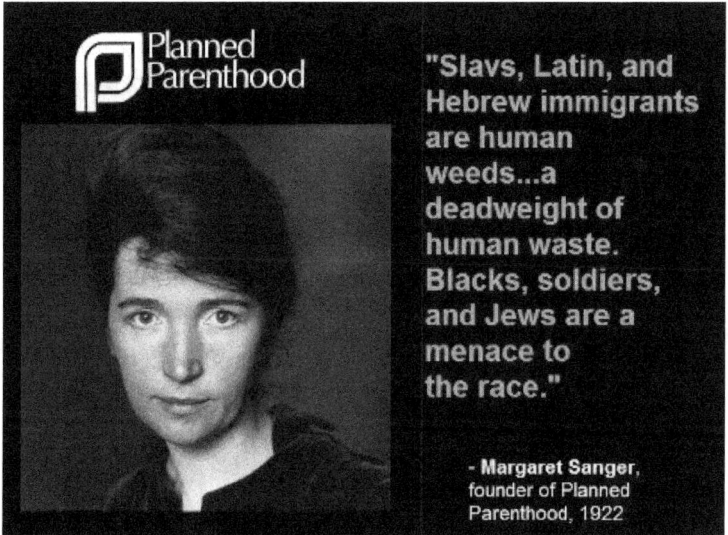

Planned Parenthood

"Slavs, Latin, and Hebrew immigrants are human weeds...a deadweight of human waste. Blacks, soldiers, and Jews are a menace to the race."

- Margaret Sanger, founder of Planned Parenthood, 1922

In the pre-World War of America Margret Sanger wrote in her book on Eugenics hate doctrines whereby she could incite the eventual advocation of abortionists to set up Planned Parenthood to do to Africans and Jews within the law exactly what Hitler and Germany was destroyed for during World War II. Hitler was quoted as saying much of his ideas in his book, he gained from reading Margret Sanger's book on Eugenics.

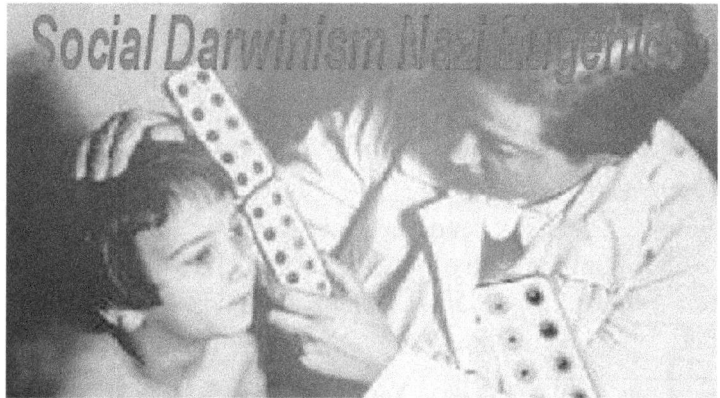

Nazi Engenics used to match eye color to ID who was a Jew

NAZI EUGENICS

Socialism
Social Darwini...
Abortio...
Genocide

Socialist Democrats, the Nazi Party used Racial features to ID Jews and those targeted for removal from the Gene-pool to create a pure ayran race.

So with this history of usage of so called Genetics and Science, it is little wonder why modern DNA science would be shunned by the Jewish people when suggestion are made that perhaps there are Jews who could discover their Jewish roots by DNA.

Many who know me as an author will know my own story on how as a child I began to have an inclination to my Mother's dismay that I was not a gentile and in fact Jewish. A Jewish friend once said to me, "Why would you want to join the club of the most hated and killed people on earth throughout all known history and time?" [11] Yet here I was, a boy with the inner drive to find my Hebrew

---

11 ***Goy Vey! I'm Jewish?*** ISBN 1479107948 EAN13: 9781479107940 ;
    ELPCo. Publishing 2012 https://www.createspace.com/3963482

Roots in DNA and in ancestry and prove that the crazy idea of some apostate from the Christian sect of pig eating Gentiles would perhaps discover some holy grail of buried truth that no one else in the family knew, or were hiding from me, that I was maybe adopted like my sister said, and from some lost tribe of Israel meant like Charlton Heston in the Ten Commandments to lead the Hebrews out of America.

After all, Jesus was Jewish was he not? So from when at 8 years old I asked the Christian Pastor "What is God's name" to the visit of the local synagogue for Holocaust Awareness and finding my name, Daniel Merrick in the list of contributors to build the Jewish building, as a young boy listening to Asa Yolson, *Al Jolson*, sing to records in Hebrew and Yiddish, something inside me, I like to call the Roauch Ha Kodesh, seemed to be telling me that I was a Jew.

So later in life, it was by design of the Abba in Heaven that loves us so and chose us to spite Tevye's dismay, and that of my own family in blindness to the facts, that I have gained a fine Jewish friend in Bernette Greenspan who happened by some unknown force (Ha Shem) to want to discover by Genetic and DNA if he and another might not have a similar Cohanim marker that could tell him who his like cousins are, and then build into his Hebrew linage and family tree, the missing parts taken away by the countless destructions and banishments of our people. [12] To me being Jewish or a Hebrew must have a DNA lineage that could be found to prove I was not crazy, just inspired.

---

12 **Faith Radio** – Bennett Greenspan Family Tree DNA
http://rdjcatalog.com/podariffic/2013/03/08/faith-radio-bennett-greenspan-family-tree-dna/ ; 2013 Hebrew Nation Radio 1220 AM Salem OR.

Zecharia 8:23 Thus saith YHUH of hosts; In those days *it shall come to pass,* that ten men shall take hold out of all languages of the nations, even shall take hold of the ZitZit *(fringe of the talliet)* of him that is a Jew, saying, We will go with you: for we have heard *that* God *is* with you.

Now the question might arise as to why this is important on this topic and subject matter, which I will gladly share with you before I move on to the next topic of understanding which I hope to prove is more fact than supposition. If I was in fact not Irish and Welsh as my parents had said, then I would have an inheritance in some land and in a family that was related to my favorite Jew at that time in my life, Yahshua Messiah who is called Jesus Christ. Further more, I had made a big mistake in the eyes of the world of Christendom, in that upon making the decision to believe in this Messiah, I started reading the Bible. The Old Testament also! So my Quest became that of inspiration in that when I read the bible from the beginning in Torah, I found out that some things around the church were not Kosher in the eyes of Ha Shem. The Idols of Tammuz in T shaped Crosses which later I found out was not in fact how this man they called by the Greek name Jesus even died. [13] I had discovered that this man was hung on a pole not the T-shape idol in the front of the church.

This all with many events in my life lead me to wonder what other lies and inaccurate information had I been given in attempts to hide my Jewish Roots?

---

13 Jerusalem Talmud page 679 blotted out texts enhanced by computer stated " They Hung Yahshua on a NACE meaning POLE on the Eve of Passover". https://www.createspace.com/4697428 Traditions Vs His Great Name 2014 ELPCo

Was it not prophesied that in the end of days or "In That Day" as the scriptures in Tanak said, that if I was a Hebrew that a long standing promise of Ha Shem would come upon me and I would discover how I had inherited lies from my forefathers, and find out I am Jewish and seek to return to the land for the final chapter of history before the Kingdom of Messiah ?

Jeremiyah 16:14-16 Therefore, behold, the days come, saith YHUH, that it shall no more be said, YHUH liveth, that brought up the children of Israel out of the land of Egypt; But, YHUH liveth, that brought up the children of Israel from the land of the north, and from all the lands whither he had driven them: and I will bring them again into their land that I gave unto their fathers. Behold, I will send for many fishers, saith YHUH, and they shall fish them; and after will I send for many hunters, and they shall hunt them from every mountain, and from every hill, and out of the holes of the rocks.

Was Ha Shem hunting for me for a greater purpose to do some great thing for Him?

As I read scriptures, both Tanak and Brit Haddasha, I found a quandary within the dogmas and doctrines of men's religion that seemed to fight against me. As Tevye said, *"on the one hand"* it seemed that for evangelical protestant Christians they had the Messiah without the Law of Torah. Somehow the message of purification or sanctification in the King James English was lost to a pardon that extended to the mistranslation of scriptures that said the ***"Law was nailed to the Cross"***.
"On the other Hand" we had the Jewish Rabbinical orders of Hasedic and Orthodox who had the Law without the Messiah. Eventually I would come to a point that would

for me be just like Tevye in the place where he is pushed to far, and at the thought of his daughter married to a Goyim not by traditions, ends the argument in his own mind with the conclusion, *"There is no other hand"*.

In 1993 to 1995 I began to search out my Genealogy and family tree which lead me to form an idea and theory that clearly my family name must have somehow survived the ages of time with a phonetic root that could be found in scriptures. It seemed that the gathering of information along with the study of the codex of names, and how surnames were in fact given to people, tribes, and found in documents, lead me to an unseen hand of Ha Shem talking to me and giving me this idea.

I then published a web site and formed an organization called the Merrick Foundation Org online and tied up with several known family members to search out my origins and document my family history in an ancestry tree. I did this to join some genealogical organizations and to preserve history of the family and the tree for my future generations. I felt this was important work to do and after retirement from the US Army this seemed a good way to use my time to benefit my family while I also worked in Mitzvah and ministry.

That is when I came to the knowledge of the Merrick name in a book by George Byron Merrick about the Family line in America written in 1902. Then I found that I had another family member who was famous for his bravery in the Civil War named also Major George Merrick. I discovered he was buried in Tioga County Pennsylvania and had made arrangements to meet a genealogist in the historical society in the county seat of that area.

I was with my wife in the car that day and as I drove to the appointment something seemed to be prompting me to pay attention to the landmarks along the way. I had heard through a long lost cousin to me, that extensive research had been done on my family line because of the founders of the first pioneers was in fact my great grandfather many generations back named Israel Merrick. As we came near the end of the journey just before turning off the road on Route 6 near the boarder of Tioga County which we had just passed, I looked and saw an old white church on the side of the road with a grave yard behind it. At that exact moment in time, like Moses seeing the burning bush, I wanted to turn aside and look at the grave stones and markers as if some hand of an angel was prompting me to stop and look. I heard a voice inside me say, "Go Look At those Stones". I said to my wife that I think we should look in that cemetery because I really feel like God is telling me that I have a relative buried there. She smiled at me as if to begin to laugh, then seeing the seriousness of my expression, she said "Let's wait until we go see the lady who we have an appointment with and we will look on the way back".

When we arrived at the Museum and Historical Society building we had all but forgotten the event which was still in my gut like a sensation of foreknowledge as if I had a vision.

When we met with the genealogist she began by sharing how she also had come from the first settlers of this area who first came on March 26th 1804 to find land and move west in the "Manifest Destiny" of the era. She went on to share that she was also a direct lineage from my Great Grandfather from seven generations back, Israel Merrick who came from Delaware, and by the way, he is buried in the Asonia Church Cemetery which just happened to be the first cemetery in the area behind the old Seventh Day Baptist Church which also served as the Sunday Baptist Church at the time when the first pioneers build it.

She went on to say that I may have passed it on the way Route 6 just before the turned off to come to see her. My wife's jaw dropped and she said, you must have been touched by an angel.

At this time in my life I started to form my theory that in fact I was not crazy, but Jewish. I published the idea on my web page that it might be helpful if someone started a Genetic Genealogy company to help trace family roots. I suggested in a paper on the site that the name Merrick was not just from Merrick, Meyrick, Myrick, Mirick, or other spellings of the phonetic codex of the name, classified as M620 in the Genealogical data, but that it was from scripture the family of Merari, son of Levi.

Genesis 46:11 And the sons of Levi; Gershon, Kohath, and **Merari.**
Numbers 26:57 And these *are* they that were numbered of the Levites after their families: of Gershon, the family of the Gershonites: of Kohath, the family of the Kohathites: of **Merari, the family of the Merarites.**

If my theory was correct, then I had not just found a phonetic language root to the Hebrew people from the Torah, but in fact I would be able to find a DNA root also. I would need DNA tests and documents to prove this.

To me it seemed prophetic that Israel Merrick was named Israel and I had a premonition that I was Jewish and from Israel as a nation of people. He had died at the very old age of 88 years 11months and 28 days. That meant he was born in 1760 just before the Revolutionary War and was 16 years old in 1776. This was significant if I was to join the National Society of Sons of the American Revolution because it meant that he was old enough to have fought in the war as many were teenagers who joined the Revolution and fought in that time for freedom from the British Crown, tax, and for the rights to worship freely according to ones own conscience.

Merari Of Merarites

In 2001 Bennett Greenspan formed a company named Family Tree DNA and had been searching out the Cohanim DNA markers for matches in his family and in efforts to link to other family members who were also searching out their Jewish DNA and Ancestry.

My theory was that the first migration of 700 BCE had caused some of the Hebrew lines to venture into Asia and move to the north into what is now Ukraine. As time passed these early Jewish travelers moved west to join into the lines and by marriages, became a part of what was first the leaders of Britannia which stretched from Germany to the west coast of Europe and the British Isles.

I found records from The Society of the Cincinnati from publications by Marjorey Lloyd Bushey Merrick who had documented the line back to 262 BCE to the line of King CoEl Codebog of the Mar which came the line of Murig and King Llewelyn of Wales. I later found that a man named George Merrick had gone south from the Pennsylvania, same name as my ancestor Major George Merrick, and that he had started a little Jewish community in the swamp lands of Florida called Coral Gables that founded the City of Miami. He was Jewish and this got my wheels turning because the biggest Jewish community in America became Miami outside of New York.

Now as evidence mounted up in on March 26th, 2001 just before the Twin Towers fell, I ordered my kit to have my DNA tested. It was not until later that I had discovered that the same day was when Israel Merrick had arrived to Delmar Township with the first pioneers in 1804.

Through some online contracts, and links to others researching the same family line such as the famous Methodist school Professor Reverend Fred Merrick, I was able to establish contacts with other Merrick family members of the same lines and find historical manuscripts that could be translated from ancient Hebrew, Greek, and Welsh and were starting to have a presence online with libraries as the Vatican Vaults were opened up in 1993 to allow for ancient Genealogies to be published. As history recorded, the line of King CoEl as in Cohen of Elohim had sent to the temple in Jerusalem to verify his right as a son of Abraham to be the first crowned King of the British people with parchments of Genealogy.

Some scholars and Genealogists doubted these documents assuming that to be King, anyone would fabricate anything to falsify their way into wealth and the crown. I disagreed with these critics and having used Biblical Genealogies, came under further criticism because of the predominant view of Evolutionary dogma taught in the universities. Some on the Genealogy web sites mocked my records and sources from every side. My father had told me as a young boy "If you are going to stick your head above the crowd, expect to get hit with tomatoes" in reference to the old vaudeville days when an act would get blasted with tomatoes to get them off the stage when the act did not preform up to par. My father had been a big fan of Al Jolson and had seen him in Pittsburgh and met him which he was very proud of being a World War II Veteran and having seen him before his tours that resulted in Jolson's lung operations. He had often as a boy gone to the old Vaudeville shows in the early 1900's and thus was a fan of many Jewish performers. He would often brag that he had seen Jolson in person and as a child I listen to

Jolson records with my dad. Deep down I wanted to be a rich and famous singer just like Al Jolson. Many in my family thought that I had some how made a type of psychological transference from listening to many of Al Jolson records with my dad when I came up with the later Idea that we were Jewish.

The family always said, like the quote from the front page of George Byron Merrick Genealogy book: "We are from the purest Cambrian blue blood, of Royal Lineage" and then they would go on with the same lines written therein "there were four brothers who came from Wales".

DESCENDANT OF KING DIES

United Press

LONDON, May 14.—Sir George Meyrick, 73, descendant of King Edward 1, died at his home in Bodorgan, Anglesey, today.

Even the United Press International had recorded our Great Uncle from the same blood line who died in 1928 as this clipping from the New York times had published that Sir George Meyrick was a descendant of King Edward I. How could I be so crazy as to think we were Jews.

little did I know at the time that I was not just fighting against family opinion, but greater religious ideas that demanded that Jews not sit here, eat here, or join this club. Further I had the Rabbis against me saying that being Jewish was not a RACE of DNA tribal identity, for these tactics were used against Jews in Germany by the Nazi's to say that Jewish was a race and not a religion. If the Rabbis were wrong, then perhaps somehow Hitler was then right in their mind. This was just to much to allow, to think that goyim were really Jews and that the Royal lines of relative to the Kings of England were in fact the Lions of the Tribe of Judah and Priests of Levi. I had gone to far.

Then as I pushed just enough to say lets look at what historical manuscripts say, the critics wrote me off and I was left in the shun list of persona not allowed to the family reunion. Now the Academia and the British Israel bunch came to odds around this time and such noted preachers as Herbert W. Armstrong of the World Wide Church of God who taught that Christians should keep the Feasts and Jewish holidays of Leviticus Chapter 23 on the Radio. He had passed away, and it seemed no advocate for my Hebrew roots theory would find me and take up my cause. Finally my DNA tests along with ancient manuscript translations came with results that would prove me crazy or a genius of prophetic proportions.

Jeremiyah 16:19 O YHUH, my strength, and my fortress, and my refuge in the day of affliction, the Gentiles shall come unto thee from the ends of the earth, and shall say, Surely our fathers have inherited lies, vanity, and *things* wherein *there is* no profit.

YDNA

The Results were in, and the amazing largest percentages of DNA matches were from Wales and Spain. The line was in fact 1.9% Wales from the Royal Kings of England and the lines went back to even Kings of European lineage. The next highest was 1.7% for Spain and that was identified as 4669 matches for Sephardic Jewish lineage. The exact markers put me into the R1b M269 group which is the same group as the Rabbis who were matches in all but 3 markers for the Cohanim Y DNA lines documented by FTDNA. The next marker was for 1.5% in Ireland that has since been proven to have been Rubenite tribal lineage. The fact is that the Armstrong hypothesis of the British being of the Brit or covenant people was in fact true.

"It would seem that those trying to promote the belief that the original Cohen and Israelite ydna Haplogroup was J downplay the significance of R1b among both Cohenim and Leviim as well as in the general population of Ashkenazi and Sephardi Jews. In order to bring down the percentage among Ashkenazim they exclude the Dutch Ashkenazi from their figures. Eupedia claims that among the Sephardi R1b is only 13 percentage when it is closer to 30 percent according to other sources. Studies on Converso descended communities show over 50 percent of R1b.

The Jewish R1b project lists many Ashkenazi Jews in the R1b haplogroup and much of it of a middle Eastern variety (Ht 35) to which many of the R1b Cohenim and Leviim belong. It is the J groups that are convert bloodlines in Judaism." [14]

"R1a1a Ashkenazi Levites who have done Y-DNA testing to date, it appears that a large proportion of Ashkenazi Jews with a tradition of Levite ancestry may share an MRCA on their direct male line who lived in the 15th century. The Y-DNA evidence and known genealogy suggest that this shared ancestor may be the founder of the

14 http://miriamhakedosha.blogspot.com/2015/04/jewish-r1b-and-haplogroup-percentages.html

Horowitz rabbinical family from Prague, Rabbi Isaiah ben Moshe Asher Halevi Horowitz (1440 – 1515 CE)."[15]

Now further when I matched up with the FTDNA family finder for matches, along with DNA matches among males, the name of Hovath, Horwitz, Katz and other known rabbinical lines show up. In addition to this information, the J1 claims to exclusive limited Y DNA markers as the Aaronic lineage is dispelled in part with the facts that the Mareri were not from the line of Aaron, yet still had the duties of Levitical priesthood in other areas of service in and around the temple. So a Cohanim or High Priest would not just be from Aarons line and DNA, but have similar Y markers within the brothers lines of Mushi, Mali, Merari and the other descendants of Levi from each generation to the next. The FTDNA Cohen model is still a match for all but 3 of my first 12 markers. The relationship charts show that I in fact have a common ancestor within 24 generations of the lines of J1 Cohen Markers, in that the R1b and R1a came from the J in a direct lineage break off from the family tree of mankind as mapped by DNA.

Each group in fact as it progressed from the proven DNA of the human tree from just one man and one woman, Adam and Eve as recorded in the Bible, the significant break off of key DNA markers is grouped into what genetic genealogist call haplogroups. So A with Adam had a break off of B and then C and so on. So R came from O that came out of J according to the present DNA models.

15 https://sites.google.com/site/levitedna/background-of-r1a1a-ashkenazi-levites

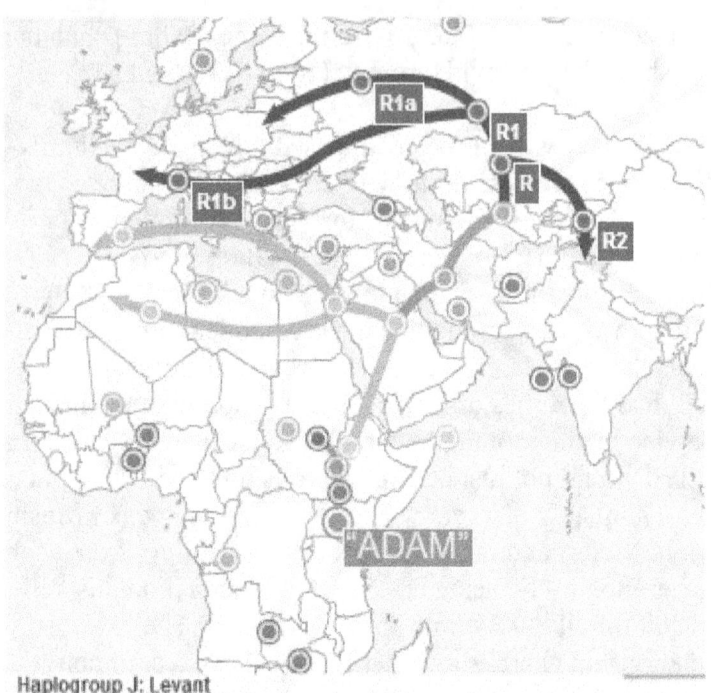

Haplogroup J: Levant
J originated in the Middle East and split into two major branches, J1 and J2.
It is a frequent haplogroup among Semitic populations.

A B C D E F G H I J K L M N O P Q R S T
View: ⦿

Yet the G is shown right were Abraham left the Ur of the Chaldea. So J came from the G and then the L which is shown in the model above to have come from G and gave rise to O from which R is said to have sprung, is in fact the same location of the first progression of the Levites of Ezra and 700 BCE who went to two locations, one east and one west near the black sea. The two R dots each side of the purple line above, shows that this is the origins of the lines. So if these were in fact the Merarites and the Josephus records showed that the J were in fact those who bought the priesthood from Rome, as Greenspan has suggested on my Radio show, then the genetic relationships would be clear in that Aaron's son's and Merari would not be from the same Y DNA markers by exact match, but would have very close relationships with only one or two markers different. That is the case with our DNA for Y R1b for the Merrick line. Both British Royalty and Merrick descendants are in fact Hebrew tribes of Merari and the Mercian lines that migrated into Europe Pre-Roman and Pre-Babylonian dispersions.

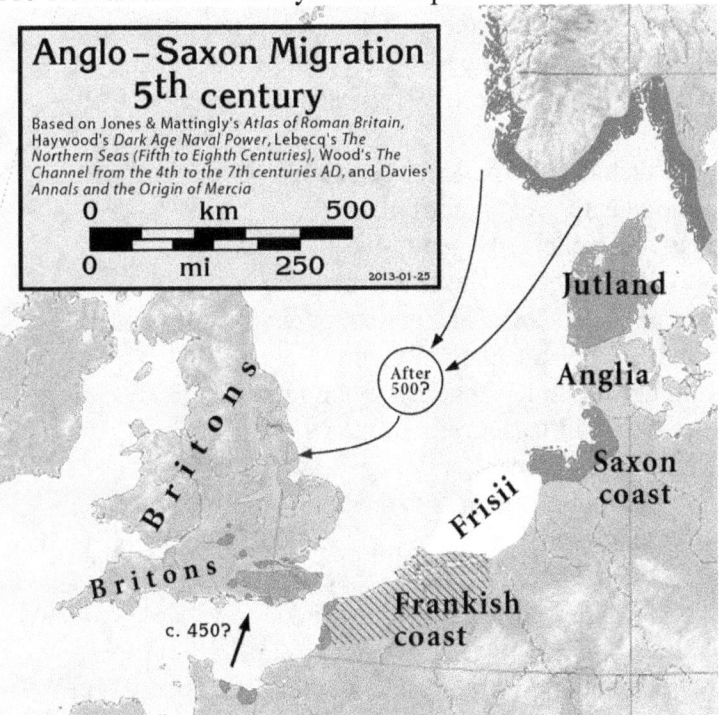

Then after the 70 CE captivity, many of the same family lines came to join relatives in England and other parts of Europe. In fact, the evidence shows that many lines of the so called lost ten tribes went to all parts of the world as prophesied would happen.

MT DNA

My MT DNA for my mother's line came back as J1b an exact match to the Cohanim from the line of Katzenellenbogen from Rabbi in Poland and in Italy where the line was carried by Rome in the 70 Titus captivity as depicted in the Arch that is still today in Rome.

Upon matching up the Genealogical data, this is my Mother's known line to which I found a multitude of cousins who died in the Holocaust.

Mordechai Katzenellenbogen (1425 -)
is your 16th great grandfather
Isaac Katzenellenbogen (1465 - 1530)
son of Mordechai Katzenellenbogen
Rabbi Isaac Meir Katzenellenbogen (1482 - 1565)
son of Isaac Katzenellenbogen
Samuel Judah Katzenellenbogen (1521 - 1597)
son of Rabbi Isaac Meir Katzenellenbogen
Saul Wahl Katzenellenbogen (1541 - 1617)
son of Samuel Judah Katzenellenbogen
"MAHARASH" MEIR WAHL KATZENELLENBOGEN
oy -- KATZENELLENBOGEN (1565 - 1630)
son of Saul Wahl Katzenellenbogen
1. Rav JUDAH WAHL KATZENELLENBOGEN
(m.Dreizel Wulff) oy -- KATZENELLENBOGEN (1599 - 1684)
son of "MAHARASH" MEIR WAHL
KATZENELLENBOGEN oy -- KATZENELLENBOGEN
Joseph Katzenellenbogen (1668 - 1739)
son of 1. Rav JUDAH WAHL KATZENELLENBOGEN
(m.Dreizel Wulff) oy -- KATZENELLENBOGEN

Agnes Katz (Katzenellenbogen) (1690 -)
daughter of Joseph Katzenellenbogen
Agnes Noltzen (1708 - 1775)
daughter of Agnes Katz (Katzenellenbogen)
Maria Barbara Steinman (1732 - 1797)
daughter of Agnes Noltzen
Christina Maurer (1763 - 1823)
daughter of Maria Barbara Steinman
Christine Elizabeth Faust Ow (1778 - 1856)
daughter of Christina Maurer
Anna Ow (1816 - 1895)
daughter of Christine Elizabeth Faust Ow
Martha Melinda Kessler (1854 - 1905)
daughter of Anna Ow
Laura Lucinda George (1881 - 1965)
daughter of Martha Melinda Kessler
Ruby Pearl Trout Sloan (1906 - 2000)
daughter of Laura Lucinda George
Laura Marie Sloan (1925 - 1998)
daughter of Ruby Pearl Trout Sloan
Daniel Walter Merrick PhD

(Source Ancestry.Com)

I also found direct matches in DNA for the South
American Sephardic MARI lines as well as the Ladino
lines with multiple matches where many had the same mix
of R1b Y DNA and J1b Mt DNA or the reverse of J for
fathers and R for mothers showing a direct relationship in
travel along the same migration paths through time.

To say the least, this did not go over big with my Irish
Catholic roots Sloan side of the family. This lead me to
find out why my mother had shushed me while we were
visiting the synagogue when I was a young boy.

A Prophet Is Without Honor

A prophet is not without honour, but in his own country, and among his own kin, and in his own house. Mark 6:4

This was a secret that no one talked about. We were Christians. Jewish lineage was a shame to talk about because they were Christ Killers. Later I found out why this attitude was expressed and not spoken of out loud.

During the early 1900's along with signs that read "Whites Only" were also the mood and discrimination of society against Jews. The signs read "No Jews Allowed" in the United States and if any hint of Jewish lineage was known, you were thrown out of the country club, church, and prohibited from attending the patronage of where others were allowed.

This year at Vacation Bible School we were to attend a Jewish Synagogue and an actual Bar Mitzvah (good works) of a young Jewish boy who had turned 13. It was part of Holocaust Awareness and the growing movement since World War Two to stop segregation in America that was becoming a movement in the United States where still some separations of blacks and Jews was still in practice. Discrimination was not just because of a race or religion, but in fact from some Communist affiliations and the facts that the Rosenberg's who were Jewish communists had given Russia secrets about the Atomic bomb. The fact that Marx was Jewish and many other factors seemed to give the white gentile Christian in America reasons to hate and separate from Jews. So at this special day during the week long summer Bible classes for young people, we would go with our parents to a Jewish Synagogue because Jesus was in fact also a Jew.

As we entered the Synagogue we were met by the Rabbi's wife who would first give us a tour and tell us of the work to document those who were lost in the Holocaust. As she spoke I stood beside my mother who was in attendance that day. The Rabbi's wife was giving a speech about the large brass plaque mounted on the front wall of the entry way that had names of those who donated to build the facilities and synagogue. Looking up at the large golden letters of names as I stood at the right side of the large list of names, I read "Daniel W Merrick" "David W Merrick" and so on.

It stuck me, THAT IS MY NAME! DANIEL W MERRICK is My Name! So I tugged on my mother's summer sun dress that she was wearing and she bent down slightly to see what I wanted and that is when I blurted out "Hey Mom, Are we Jews, Look There's my name". At that moment I saw fear in my mother's eyes which I did not understand until long after her passing. She shushed me and said in a soft voice, "We'll talk about this later". We never did until a few years before she died when she said only that her Great Grandmother had been Jewish.

Never in all my days with my Grandmother Sloan or my Mother was this talked about openly. It was fear that had driven them to hide the past in ancestry that was in our DNA. We did not talk about this because in America it had been carefully hidden from public knowledge that some of these lines from the Mayflower to today were in fact, JEWS. They did not want to be labeled Jewish and Christ Killers and prevented from going out to eat or even worse, to get beaten or killed because of who our relatives were.

In the 1947 film *"Gentleman's Agreement"* Actor Gregory Peck has one line near the end of the film that when I first heard it, lead me to research more about what I had felt for years the Holy Spirit was telling me. The line from the script in the film was

"We all think we're white Christian Merricks' "

Still at that time in History it was not public knowledge of the famous film producer David Merrick having not just a Jewish Religion, but in fact, a Hebrew name. The Merrick name had been long in America and had been an established WASP name from the shores of Wales and England until the Coming of the four Royal brothers in 1636 on the Good Ship James. William, James, John and Thomas were all from the Protestant ministry lineage of the Right Roland D Merrick and Rev John Merrick who were in fact cousins to the King and from their common Great Grandparent King Edward the First.

So in the Film when Peck says it like is is understood in modern American Society that these Protestant founders of this country would be a stereotype of the perfect gentile Christian understanding of the day used to allow us to keep silent in the face of Antisemitic acts, jokes, and discrimination, all society understands his reference to my family name "Merrick".

As a young eight year old, these things started to come to light inside me, that I was feeling like I was Jewish and that it was important to my life that I knew this, recognized it, and was not afraid to say what I thought. The fact that this was hidden and unprovable made no difference to me. In my mind Jesus was a Jew and so was I. Even though the family was from Wales, I was reminded this when I would say, "we are in fact Jewish". I could feel it in my bones and the Holy Spirit seemed to be leading me to a Jewish perspective of things as I fell in love with Messiah and his ways.

In the last 15 years of my life, I have found that the move of the Spirit of the Almighty was not just moving me to see the importance of being a Jew to my spiritual life, but that even more than that, the fact that I was a Jew proved that the Torah Law, if "Just for the Jews" as some Christians said, was in fact for me also because I was a Jew. Recently I have found lots of these pictures on Facebook that show some Christians are beginning to get a clue about the fact that I saw as a child, that Yahshua who they call Jesus, is and was a Jew.

The truth about the Hebrew roots of Christianity is now becoming a popular message and one that comes in lines with much of the real new testament teaching of a spiritual understanding of FAITH that holds to the fact that those who are not the seed of Jacob by DNA are grafted into Israel by doctrine from the first followers of Christ who wrote this:

***Letter to the Romans 11:17** And if some of the branches be broken off, and thou, being a wild olive tree, wert graffed in among them, and with them partakest of the root and fatness of the olive tree; (Rabbi Sha'ul of Tarsas)*

The Olive tree rich with oil is Israel and the Jewish people and that ones who are grafted in are the Gentiles who would by Torah law become under the same law as Israel by FAITH.

***Amos 9:12** "...and of all the Gentiles, which are called by my name, saith YHUH that doeth this.*

It seems that the common faith of what saves us has become in these last days clear to the Christians who support Israel and who seek to embrace truth over the lies of history, that if one name is how we are saved in the Tanak and in the Brit Haddasha, then prehaps one family is also who we should be supporting and fighting for. There is only two groups listed on the present terrorists hit list, the Great Satan and the Little Satan. That is how the Christian United States and the Nation of Israel is more in common than apart. As Genesis says: "I will bless those who bless you, and curse those who curse you" speaking of the Hebrew people.

Joel 2:32 And it shall come to pass, that whosoever shall call on the name of YHUH shall be delivered: for in mount Zion and in Jerusalem shall be deliverance, as YHUH hath said, and in the remnant whom YHUH shall call. (Tanak)

Romans_10:13 For whosoever shall call upon the name of YHUH shall be saved. (Brit Haddasha)

So in fact we are in agreement as Jews and Christians, and it seems with terrorist, under the same gun of hate in recent times.

So I came to the conclusion like Tevye that *"There is no other hand".* If Israel is my seed, and the Torah is the law for Jews, then even if I believed in Messiah as Yahshua who the Hebrew Rabbis rejected, i would still be required to keep the FAITH in the one true Elohim and follow His commandments to the best of my ability.

Many Messianic Jewish and Christian groups with DNA proven Jewish people are of late flocking to keep the feasts that were before shunned for pagan celebrations. So it seems logical that if the Roauch Ha Kodesh was leading me to find my Jewish roots, then it also was teaching me that the law of doing good and righteousness in keeping Sabbath and following the moral codes of the Jews was not in opposition to who I was by Faith or DNA. So if the Jews had the law with man made traditions without the Messiah and the Christians had the Messiah without the Law and also man made pagan traditions, then neither was by my more Karite view, that had developed in me, that of the scriptural stand. Yet still no reason to forsake my Hebrew family for a pig dinner on Sunday.

The bottom line for me boiled down to one fact, either I was right and Messiah was Yahshua who most men call Jesus, or I was wrong and the Messiah is still yet to come. All the anti-missionaries from Judaism and Catholic Priests in Rome could not change my mind on these facts. So if I escaped the lawless Christian doctrine for a more balanced Torah observant doctrine, then my keeping sabbath as a Jew would prove me at least as worthy as a righteous Gentile, and if I was right and Yahshua is Messiah, perhaps my being a Jew would show that the common Faith in the name of Ha Shem to my Jewish brothers and sisters would at least get me in the door to share what I had discovered. I might even get some Kallah and Wine.

Now I do not deny my Jewish Messiah, I teach and preach in His Name each week on my Radio Show entitled FAITH RADIO. Yet I have not compromised with my new found FAITH to think that the Almighty did not mean what He said when Exodus 20 says NO IDOLS OF ANYTHING either. So I do not hold to the bowing to Idols of the Cross when if it was how Messiah died it would be the equal of bowing to a shotgun if He had been shot. It is nice though to see some Christians wake up.

Through the years I have made great Jewish friends such as Avi Lipkin, Nehemia Gordon, and my bother-in-law who lives in Ashdod. Yet the only thing I would like from the Orthodox Rabbis in Israel would be a right to come home when they let in Messianic's like me, or at least the acknowledgment that there is a DNA line of the Seed of people who crossed the river Jordan to move into the Promise land and it might be better for both of us if we stick together in these troubling times.

So I do not agree that "Jewish" is a religion, I think "Jewish" or more correctly being Hebrew is a family by seed and DNA that has promises from the Almighty in scriptures to which I also by DNA and seed have an inheritance to the land as my home.

Terms Of Endearment

Desposyni (Greek δεσπόσυνοι, desposynoi, "those of the master") is a term used uniquely by Sextus Julius Africanus[35] to refer to the relatives of Jesus. The Gospels mention four brothers of Jesus—James, Joses, Simon, and Jude[94]—along with two sisters, named by Epiphanius[95] as Mary and Salome (or Anna and Salome).[96] https://en.wikipedia.org/wiki/Genealogy_of_Jesus

Kahmari: Term used to denote the close relatives of the blood lines of those associated family members of the levitical lines of the mother of Mary from the tribe of Levi. Kah is a chaldean word for Spirit, Mari is the line of worship leaders of Levi that played music from the scriptures in
1Ch_6:47 The son of Mahli, the son of Mushi, the son of Merari, the son of Levi. 1Ch 23:5 Moreover four thousand were porters; and four thousand praised the LORD with the instruments which I made, said David, to praise therewith.
1Ch 23:6 And David divided them into courses among the sons of Levi, namely, Gershon, Kohath, and Merari.
2Ch_34:12 And the men did the work faithfully: and the overseers of them were Jahath and Obadiah, the Levites, of the sons of Merari; and Zechariah and Meshullam, of the sons of the Kohathites, to set it forward; and other of the Levites, all that could skill of instruments of musick.

The Family name Merrick came from the mixture in Europe of Merari and Musickah from the area of Ukraine after the dispersion found in Ezra in the bible. The sons had married gentile women and were put out of the

41

Assyrian return and moved north into what is now Afghanistan and Ukraine about 700BC. The words for Music in Russian and Ukrainian language was Musickah denoting the Kah of the Spirit and the use of music in worship. The combination of the
words for the tribe of Levi which was Merari the son of Levi became Mer-ic-kah for the Merarites who played Music. The Merari were not son's of Aaron, so they did not have the title of Cohanim Gadol or High Priest but being of Levi had the duties of carrying the outer temple poles, curtains, and other parts of the tent which made up the temple. They also played the worship music and carried the instruments for worship. When King Henry the 7th first made surnames for those of the British Isles they also knew of those who were from Royal lines from David and the tribes of Merari and Levi, and thus appropriately named the sons of the lines by the fathers before them.

The original word for the tribe of Levi in ancient Hebrew was in fact Lewite (Leu White) which is the phonetic root of the word for Louie and Llewellyn the king by that name in Wales. The phonetic soundex system was created for genealogists to group surnames into similar sounding names coming from a same common ancestor. For Merrick the Codex #M620 (Jewish Gen Code-M code 695000 or 694500) is used to identify the lines that came from the earliest known ancestor as in Wales as Merrick son of Llewellyn who was also called Murig. The associated line of Mawr, Mar, Merari, and Mir with phonetic Mer and Zimmer or Zimmar taken also from the instrument of the same name believed to have been a type of harp in ancient times. In Germanic form the ZA or THE and MAR for Merarite. From these progressions of the name came the word Singer also.

In America the house of John Merrick of the Virginia Company of London held indentured servants in exchange for passage to the new world. For seven years half of all the crops and earnings came to the company in payment for freedom.

As a result of this begrudging over this contract after the fact, it became common slang to call the country "A Merrick A" because of owing half of all to the Merrick family company. The Italian Roman Catholic Church claimed that the man name Amerigo had first claimed to discover this new world and that it was the reason for this name. Later the fraud was discovered that Amerigo had not traveled to the new world yet the Roman Catholic Author's of books seemed to continue to rewrite history in favor of this liar as the one who discovered America. Yet the Merrick Indians were also among the first contacts after 1492 when Columbus came to the new world and they held that phonetic name for over one thousand years. The recent studies in DNA have shown that the Merrick Native American tribes along with the Seneca and Cherokee have roots in the Hebrew Tribal lineage. Artifacts found in the burial mounds of Ohio have been proven to have the sacred name of God in Hebrew, the letters Y-H-U-H on them and the Cherokee word for the Great Spirit is "Hey Yah Who Way AH" similar in sound to Yahuah and Yahweh. DNA matching has proven that the Egyptian and Hebrew lines are mixed into the native American tribes.

This was discovered when Dr Davies of Oxford found that Nicotine and Coca were in all the mummies and the chemical compounds were used in ancient embalming. The pattern of Evidence shows that the Hebrews in slavery in Egypt, came in ships to the Americas to gather tobacco and Coca leaves which were used in the mummification process. No doubt, now by DNA proven, some ships did not survive the journey and the stranded people became cultivators of plants and remained in the Americas finding freedom there before the time of Christ. The resulting inner-marriage of the Amer-asians became what are known as native American tribes. When one looks at the Egyptian and Hebrew influences found in burial practice and pyramid like tombs along with the ancient Hebrew words for the name of God, this fact can not be disputed.

I have no doubt that this country was name for the Merari Hebrew who first came here and named it such. Along with the folklore of the Merrick Virginia Company being in distaine for it's part in slavery for passage, the resulting mockery of "A Merrick Ah" became a type of phonetic history repeating itself.

Merarite Clan

"The Merarites were given twelve cities from the tribes of Zebulun, Reuben, and Gad. Their city allotment can be found in Joshua 21:34-40. From the tribe of Zebulun Jokneam, Kartah, Kimnah, Nahalal From the tribe of Reuben Bezer, Jahaz, Kedemoth, Mephaath From the tribe of Gad Ramoth-Gilead, a city of refuge, Mahanaim, Heshbon, Jazer In all, the tribe of Levi received a total of forty-eight towns in the "territory held by the Israelites". Only 9 rested south of Jerusalem. The heartland of Israel, Judah, Ephraim, and Manasseh, did not receive the majority of Levitical cities. Rather, most cities lie in the peripheral areas to the north and east of the heartland.

Much of the area encompassed by these cities of the tribe of Levi lie within Canaanite controlled territory until the time of David. Indeed, God's presence was needed most in these areas under idolatrous influence. Not only did the tribe of Levi receive these cities, but Scripture indicates they also received the pasture lands surrounding each town as well. Numbers 35 records an interesting conversation between God and Moses. God instructs Moses on how each city given to the tribe of Levi is to be structured. God's attention to detail is incredible. Each Levite town has pasture lands for "their cattle, flocks and all their other livestock".

The pasture lands around each town are to extend fifteen hundred feet from the town wall. Three thousand feet are allotted for each pastureland, on each side of the city: 3,000 ft. on the east side; 3,000 ft. on the south side; 3,000 ft. on the west side; and 3,000 ft. on the north side. The town itself was to rest in the center, surrounded on each side by huge pastures. The Levites were to be self-sufficient, relying solely on God for sustenance. God, in turn, provided each city with enough cattle, flocks, livestock, land, and crops to be self-reliant. Each of the tribes of Israel, in essence, paid a tithe to God; in the form of towns and land, within their respective tribal allotment. These were to be given specifically to the tribe of Levi."

Published in 1847 by John Wright Printer, The History of the Tribe of Levi Considered is an in-depth study in into the tribe of Levi.

It is believed and shown by DNA today in many studies that the Jews who were from France and Spain of some note as Sephardic lines, had come to be known as the MAR, Maritie and even by name Mari.

Abba Mari ben Moses ben Joseph Astruc

"Abba Mari ben Moses ben Joseph Astruc was a 14th century Jewish scholar in Montpellier. He was appalled at the willingness of many Jewish scholars to explain the Torah rationally. They even maintained that certain Torah images were allegories and metaphors. In a scathing work, Sefer HaYareach, Astruc emphasized traditional rabbinic beliefs.

He initiated the third attack against Maimonides' Guide For the Perplexed, initiating a major Maimonidean Controversy. He succeeded in convincing Solomon ben Abraham Adret to issue a ban against anyone who studied the text before the age of twenty-five. This ban was taken further in Provence, prohibiting the study of science, metaphysics, rational explanations for the Torah, and philosophical interpretations of midrash and aggadah. In 1306, the Jews (including Astruc) were expelled from France. He ended up in Perpignan where he settled."[16]

Barbados

The history of the Jews in Barbados has existed almost continually since 1654, when Sephardic Jews arrived on the island as refugees from Dutch Brazil. The Jewish refugees brought with them expertise in the production and cultivation of sugarcane and coffee, expertise which contributed to the development of Barbados as a major producer of sugar.[17]

---

16 www.jewishvirtuallibrary.org/jsource/biography/Astruc.html
17 https://en.wikipedia.org/wiki/History_of_the_Jews_in_Barbados

Among the many records is found also the coming of William Merrick one of the four brothers who also was known to have a large sugar plantation in Barbados. The history of names found there in many books of the era from the late 1500's to 1700's show a tie that is without dispute among both historians and genealogists.

The matches of DNA on family finder with FTDNA and other connections by those in Brazil and in known Sephardic communities has proven the lineage of this family and associations by heritage. These lines came from Spain during the years of the inquisition and along with Columbus even made way with the first who discovered America with him. [18]

The records prove that many of the first who came to American shores were in fact Israelite by heritage and DNA. Among these were the Mari by surname and the Merari by first biblical surname if we consider the lines that they came from.

Dating Bias

The Time Line Errors of Genealogical Evolutionist is not unlike that of those in Archaeology who hold that the Exodus is off by 400 years given their estimations and dating methods. In a recent film about the Exodus this grave error is exposed and proven by the bias of those who ignore all the archaeology clues found in Egypt and even those found at the bottom of the Red Sea. If these who hold to evolution admit their error, they would also

---

18 http://www.britannica.com/topic/Diaspora-Judaism ; The Four Blood Moons, history of Sephardic contributions to Christopher Columbus and his voyage in 1492.

have to admit there is in fact a God who by divine power set the people of Israel free from slavery with miracles. This is also the case with the dating of the Mari which evolutionary biased men claim happened prior to Abraham and therefore have even influenced the Encyclopedia Judaica to alter it's previous historical account of the group of Mari as being a pre-abrahamic Semitic race. Their time line predates Abraham by 20,000 years which we know is not just an error, but a preexistence of earth by the correct biblical time line.

The facts are that the Merari and Levi were from Abraham not the other way around as they claim. If the Mari by DNA have Semitic genetics then they are from the same lines biologically. So I would rather agree with the biblical view which takes these same matches and dates them more in line with the records of genealogical lines from the bible.

So when we find Y DNA for the male lines matching from these far eastern Arabian lines, to assume that the later lineage was from the former Mari, who match in markers with Males of the J and R makers of these haplogroups, is to attempt to put the cart before the horse. The R1b Merari lines from Merrick match with Mari lines who have J and with cohanim who are also J groups. The number of different markers in the first 12 are only 2 or 3 and show a common ancestor within 40 generations. Yet when the base lines in the males are compared at full sequences of markers, we find a root common ancestor at about 70 to 80 generations. This is important because if we take a generation by father to son to grandson are about 50 years we can see when these common fathers actually walked the earth with a bit of math. 20 generations of 50 years

48

would be 1000 years. So to get to Abraham at 3500 years we get about 70 generations. So if these samples match in DNA then they could not have come before Abraham. The R1b and R1a lines in close relationship by Markers in DNA are proven as relatives of J1b who have Cohanim lines. In fact they are so close in relationship by makers, only one or two in most cases are different. When matched with the Mari line that came to South America we find still the same relationship. So if we accept the Evolutionary model of mankind's family tree time line we find that the actual time line would not fit. The 20,000 year mutation rate would have left them with differences that would have left half of the Y markers replaced with other longer divergence. The evolutionist line is at 400 generations. From Adam to present day man is only about 105 to 120 generations. We know this because when we date bible texts and parchments along with archaeological items associated with these historical individuals we get the 70 generations to Abraham. We do the same with other known persons from the bible and get Babylonian artifacts and Daniel the Prophet and find this same matching time line effect. So to take then a known phonetic surname origin and then change it to not sync with ancestry methods would be foolish and show the bias to dispute the creation of man with the fable of monkey mutations magically turning into humans.

The is also the Barbados foot print of DNA that remains with both the South American Maria and the Merrick of North America that shows records of marriage into lines that show the R1b and R1a associated lines are common with Horvath, Meyer, Katz, and other lines who have varied R, J, and H lines that could not be so if they all had a predominant male Y line that was a single great grandfather. If they had that common ancestor then they would have had the same haplogrouping under that common grandfather. We see this in maps of lines of haplogroups and how each broke off from the previous line. Thus even with the evolutionary model they place Adam and Eve as the genetic source of all mankind. They put their Adam and Eve at 50,000 years ago. We put them in biblical line of time at 6000 years ago which matches our records and ancestry lines in time and generations. So it is impossible for their Mari from 20,000 to have been before the first man even existed. So this proves that Mari was from Merari in the bible and the DNA in the Male Y lines proves they are related across Haplgroups.

Further more the evolutionist's time line puts mankind at 1,000 generations. Given the known history of man at 6,000 years with presently 7 billion people on the planet, we can not agree. If we take into account the graves alone that this exaggerated number would predict with a simple math formula, the archaeological record in the earth proves this to be an error of grave proportions. (Pun intended). Given the natural culling of mankind by natural disasters, diseases, and war just to name a few, if we take the present 7 billion as a fair estimation of growth in procreation, 50,000 divided by 6,000 equals 8.33 So if we then use our present population to multiply by 7 billion we would have about 58.4 billion people on the planet. Besides the food problem and space problem that would cause, it also tells us that the 1,000 generation theory is not just wrong, but impossible.

If we take the same math and figure in an actual evolutionary primal man with unchecked sexual instincts coming from animals, then you see how ridicules it is to think we evolved over millions of years because the amounts of population would be beyond our ability to have survived this long. Even one million years of generations would be 166.6 and the population would be that times 7 billion which would have destroyed all resources long ago and mankind would not exist today with over 1 trillion 166 billion people from such a model of progression of procreation.

The Kah'Mari Desposyni

The Kah' Mari Desposyni are those who are of the line of Merari and Aaron of the tribe of Levi or Lewites who are relatives of the Messiah Yahshua. The related family tree is below showing the relationship of Judah and the line of Cohanim priesthood through the cousins of Marium mother of Yahshua.

Many teachers and readers have not a clue what this means and why it is important. To understand and be filled with JOY and make you jump up and down like I did when I discovered this, you need to know about PROMISES that YAHUAH made and why this is important for the reasons of the SEED.

Gen_12:7 And YAHUAH appeared unto Abram, and said, Unto thy seed will I give this land: and there builded he an altar unto YAHUAH, who appeared unto him.

Exo_32:13 Remember Abraham, Isaac, and Israel, thy servants, to whom thou swarest by thine own self, and saidst unto them, I will multiply your seed as the stars of heaven, and all this land that I have spoken of will I give unto your seed, and they shall inherit it for ever.

Gen_14:18 And Melchizedek king of Salem brought forth bread and wine: and he was the priest of the most high God.

Psa_76:2 In Salem also is his tabernacle, and his dwelling place in Zion.

Heb 7:1-3 For this Melchisedec, king of Salem, priest of the most high God, who met Abraham returning from the slaughter of the kings, and blessed him; To whom also Abraham gave a tenth part of all; first being by interpretation King of righteousness, and after that also King of Salem, which is, King of peace; Without father, without mother, without descent, having neither beginning of days, nor end of life; but made like unto the Son of God; abideth a priest continually.

first being by interpretation King of righteousness, and after that also King of Salem, which is, King of peace

When Yahshua Messiah came he first came as the LAMB to take away the sins of the world and be KING OF RIGHTEOUSNESS to us all.

AFTER THAT he became the HIGH PRIEST in the Atonement of His Blood in the Ark in Heaven and He is coming back as KING OF PEACE to bring Two things together that had never before been together in the same person in Israel.

That is, He is both KING of the line of DAVID and PRIEST of the line of AARON from LEVI by promise in scripture and the words of the prophets to bring it to HIS SEED for the Inheritance as YAH PROMISED.

In the Brit Hadasha Matthew gives the line of Joseph and Luke the line of Marium or Mary the earthly parents of Yahshua Messiah.

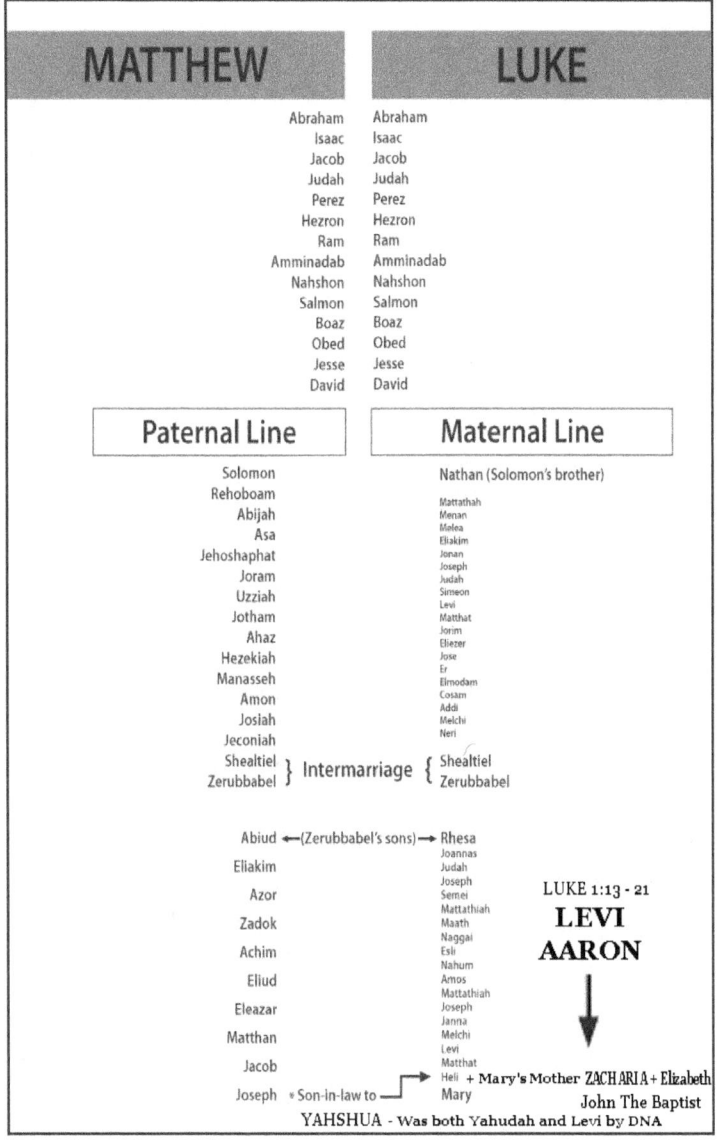

So we have two accounts of the Messiah and his DNA SEED line by Genealogy. So lets look at LUKE and other scriptures to see how this lines up with the prophetic MELECH ZADEICH which means KING of RIGHTEOUSNESS.

As a side note, these also from MARI by surname also can trace their lines to Messiah Yahshua and Rabbincal as well as Messianic Jewish lines. The relationship to Yahshua is not a religious relationship but a DNA genetic one so many from practicing Judaism found in Spanish South American Sephardic lines have related surnames as well as those in North America and Europe such as:

Maria, Merrick, Meyrick, Sloan, Fox, Hoff, Hardie, Pehlem, Meyrick, Myrick, Chapman, and many others listed in our Ancetry Family Tree at Ancestry.Com and on the web sites at Family tree DNA.

So when we look at the chart or Family Tree below we find these were relatives by seed and DNA of Heli of Judah by Mrs Heli, here father who was named Aaron, and the relatives of also the line of Elizabeth and Zacharia parents of John the baptist. The lines from Levi and Aaron through both the Cohanim priesthood as well as Merari though such lines as Joseph of Arimathaea, being a disciple of Yahshua as recorded in John 19:38 who was in fact related to Aaron the father of Elizabeth.

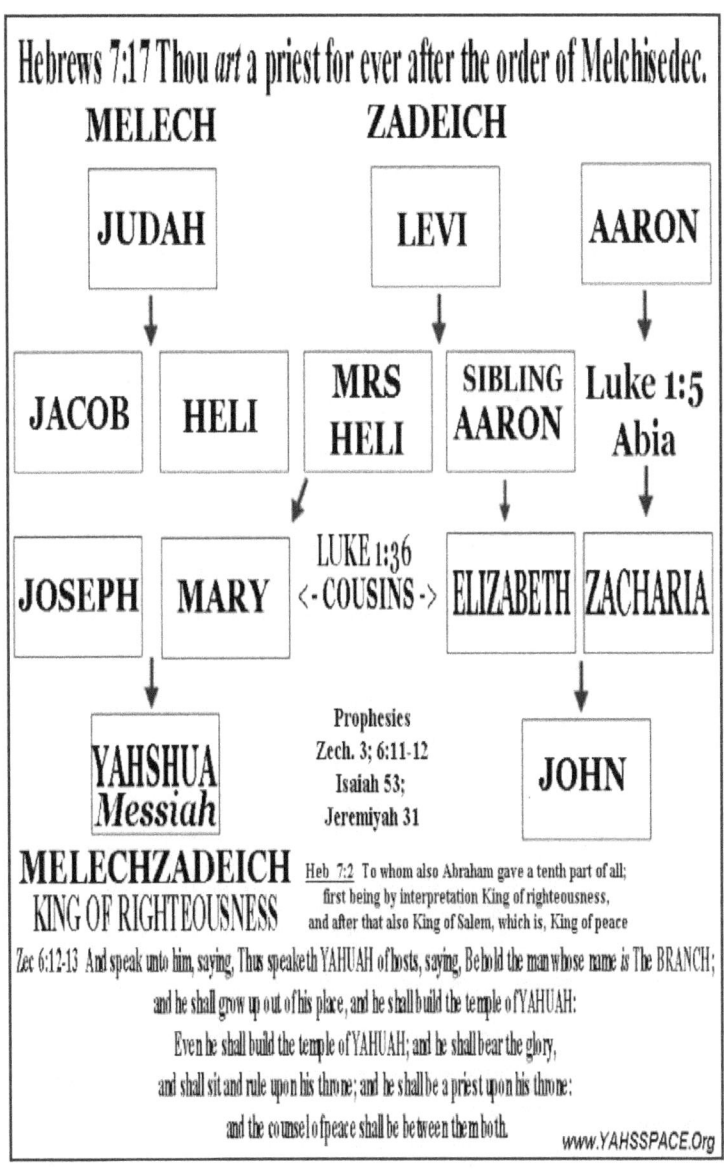

Hebrews 7:17 Thou *art* a priest for ever after the order of Melchisedec.

MELECH **ZADEICH**

JUDAH **LEVI** **AARON**

JACOB **HELI** **MRS HELI** **SIBLING AARON** Luke 1:5 Abia

JOSEPH **MARY** LUKE 1:36 <‑COUSINS‑> **ELIZABETH** **ZACHARIA**

YAHSHUA *Messiah*

Prophesies
Zech. 3; 6:11-12
Isaiah 53;
Jeremiah 31

JOHN

MELECHZADEICH
KING OF RIGHTEOUSNESS

Heb 7:2 To whom also Abraham gave a tenth part of all; first being by interpretation King of righteousness, and after that also King of Salem, which is, King of peace

Zec 6:12-13 And speak unto him, saying, Thus speaketh YAHUAH of hosts, saying, Behold the man whose name *is* The BRANCH; and he shall grow up out of his place, and he shall build the temple of YAHUAH:

Even he shall build the temple of YAHUAH; and he shall bear the glory,

and shall sit and rule upon his throne; and he shall be a priest upon his throne:

and the counsel of peace shall be between them both.

www.YAHSSPACE.Org

The SCRIPTURES tell us that Elizabeth is cousin of Mary and that Elizabeth is the daughter of Aaron who is married to Zacharia who is a Priest of LEVI under the Abia course of duty in the Temple.

That means by TORAH LAW that the PRIEST can only marry within the TRIBE of LEVI.

MRS HELI is mother of Mary and she not being a priest since only men were, could marry outside the tribe. She married into JUDAH as a tribe when she married HELI.

That means that the MT DNA of MESSIAH was both JUDAH and LEVI by inheritance. So when Zechariah in chapter 6 prophesies of the COUNSEL OF PEACE BETWEEN THEM BOTH he is speaking of TWO Offices of leadership being KING and PRIEST. "He Shall sit upon his throne a priest"

MELLECH is KING, ZADEIC is RIGHTEOUSNESS. Melchizedek is the combination of these two words.

So by DNA rights and prophesied inheritance the PRIESTHOOD of AARON and LEVI was transferred to MESSIAH when the Vail of the Temple was torn in TWO. The KINGDOM of ISRAEL will be transferred to MESSIAH when He Returns as both KING and PRIEST.

Melchizedek Yahusha Yahushua Messiah.

When you see this by both Spirit and Truth, Genealogy and Promise, by SEED and by all that is involved in the Anointing of the Roauch Ha Kodesh, you see the JOY of the Messiah INSIDE YOU!

Jer 31:31 Behold, the days come, saith YAHUAH, that I will make a new covenant with the house of Israel, and with the house of Judah:
Jer 31:32 Not according to the covenant that I made with their fathers in the day that I took them by the hand to bring them out of the land of Egypt; which my covenant they brake, although I was an husband unto them, saith

YAHUAH:

Jer 31:33 But this shall be the covenant that I will make with the house of Israel; After those days, saith YAHUAH, I will put my law in their inward parts, and write it in their hearts; and will be their God, and they shall be my people.

Jer 31:34 And they shall teach no more every man his neighbour, and every man his brother, saying, Know YAHUAH: for they shall all know me, from the least of them unto the greatest of them, saith YAHUAH: for I will forgive their iniquity, and I will remember their sin no more.

Jer 31:35 Thus saith YAHUAH, which giveth the sun for a light by day, and the ordinances of the moon and of the stars for a light by night, which divideth the sea when the waves thereof roar; YAHUAH of hosts is his name:

Jer 31:36 If those ordinances depart from before me, saith YAHUAH, then the seed of Israel also shall cease from being a nation before me for ever.

Jer 31:37 Thus saith YAHUAH; If heaven above can be measured, and the foundations of the earth searched out beneath, I will also cast off all the seed of Israel for all that they have done, saith YAHUAH.

Jer 31:38 Behold, the days come, saith YAHUAH, that the city shall be built to YAHUAH from the tower of Hananeel unto the gate of the corner.

Jer 31:39 And the measuring line shall yet go forth over against it upon the hill Gareb, and shall compass about to Goath.

Jer 31:40 And the whole valley of the dead bodies, and of the ashes, and all the fields unto the brook of Kidron, unto the corner of the horse gate toward the east, shall be holy unto YAHUAH; it shall not be plucked up, nor thrown down any more for ever.

When the ROAUCH comes into us, we are the TEMPLE of YAHUAH for WORSHIP of HIS NAME with JOY.

KING OF RIGHTEOUSNESS is INSIDE US as the scriptures say. The PROMISE to the SEED and the Gentiles that are CALLED BY HIS NAME are one in the NEW ISRAEL of ISRAYAH by POWER of YAH to overcome all sin, all evil, all wickedness, all sickness, all lies, all slander, all failure to do the will of Yahuah and that is why we are making our requests known before HIM who LOVES US and GAVE HIMSELF FOR US.

The RULE by SEED and GRANT by PRIESTHOOD merged into ONE MESSIAH and that is why as a JUDAH and LEVI from Merari I am so filled with JOY at KNOWING THIS. That I have such a cousin that can take the inheritance by the SEED and by the RULE and by the SPIRIT and by the ANOINTING and by HIS CREATION use us to do some righteousness in this world by HIS STRENGTH. Why do I love him so, because HE SAVED ME and SHOWED ME this purpose to share HIS SALVATION with the world.

70 generations ago my grandfather we a LEVITE on my father's side, and from the Grandfather of YAHSHUA MESSIAH MATTHAT where my mother's line from YAHUDAH came. This makes me the 1st Cousin of Yahshua Messiah 70 generations removed. YET NOT REMOVED FROM ME FOR HE LIVES INSIDE ME.

So the seed of the promise for the land is not just to me to dwell there with him, but to dwell in His Kingdom which he has inherited by the promise for me, that I might live in righteousness in the body of Messiah as His Bride. AND YOU ALSO who hear and believe on HIS NAME and CALL ON HIM for Salvation are part of what is about to

58

happen to this earth and all the house of ISRAEL shall be SAVED with the GENTILES CALLED BY HIS NAME gathered into ONE PLACE for HIS ETERNAL PURPOSE.

So when we see these things come to be, with Prophesy coming true, with Israel at the brink and Iran sending troops to Syria and Russia allied with Persia as prophets have foretold, I FIND JOY in the FEAR OF YAHUAH that I pray for all to be saved and call on HIS NAME for the DAY IS SHORT.

Worship HIS the MELECH ZADEICH YAHUSAH YAHSHUA MESSIAH and YAHUAH for this is the day when all the prophets longed to see, when two witnesses shall come, when Antimessiah and Ha Satan will be destroyed, when all idols will be cast away into the fires and all places that keep idols will be pounded into dust.

NO MORE will you need to say to your neighbor DO YOU KNOW THE NAME OF YAHUAH, for it shall be on the Bells on the Horses and no cooking pot shall be unclean with pig any more. ON the POTS AND PANS will be written SACRED AND PURE UNTO YAHUAH.

MALE MERRICK, Codex #M620 (Jewish Gen Code-M code 695000 or 694500)Genealogy: Male Merrick Lineage from : Yah, GOD: To be praised, honored, and glorified forever Creator of the first man- As Recorded in First Chronicles 1:1;1:24-28: Genesis1: Adam & Eve 4000 BC

The Kah'Mari Desposyni from Scriptures

Matthew 1:2-16

Abraham begat Isaac
Isaac begat Jacob
Jacob begat Judas and his brethren;
Judas begat Phares and Zara of Thama
Phares begat Esrom
Esrom begat Aram
Aram begat Aminadab
Aminadab begat Naasson
Naasson begat Salmon
Salmon begat Booz of Rachab
Booz begat Obed of Ruth
Obed begat Jesse
Jesse begat David the king
David the king begat Solomon of Bathsheba that had been
the wife of Urias
olomon begat Roboam
Roboam begat Abia
Abia begat Asa
Asa begat Josaphat
Josaphat begat Joram
Joram begat Ozias
Ozias begat Joatham
Joatham begat Achaz
Achaz begat Ezekias
Ezekias begat Manasses
Manasses begat Amon
Amon begat Josias
Josias begat Jechonias and his brethren, about the time
they were carried away to Babylon
And after they were brought to Babylon,
Jechonias begat Salathiel
Salathiel begat Zorobabel
Zorobabel begat Abiud
Abiud begat Eliakim

Eliakim begat Azor
Azor begat Sadoc
Sadoc begat Achim
Achim begat Eliud
Eliud begat Eleazar
Eleazar begat Matthan
Matthan begat Jacob;
Jacob begat Joseph the husband of Marium (Mary) of
whom was born
Yahshua who is called Messiah (Jesus, who is called
Christ.)

The Merrick Connection:

Matthat som of Levi (Luke 3:23-38 below)
JOSEPH Ben MATTHAT Mathhonwy ARIMATHEA (38
- 82)
son of Aaron Ben Levi by lineage, or the line of Cohanim
Gadol or High Priest.
Enygeus Ann Ben Joseph (Spokenn in BIble)
daughter of JOSEPH Ben MATTHAT Mathhonwy
ARIMATHEA
Caradoc of Siluria
son of Enygeus Ann Ben Joseph (Spokenn in BIble)
Cyllinus King of Siluria Mawr (99 - 142)
son of Caradoc of Siluria
Old King Coel Mawr (108 - 158)
son of Cyllinus King of Siluria Mawr
Lleiffer Mawr King of Colchester (137 - 221)
son of Old King Coel Mawr
Gwladys Ferch Lleiffer Mawr (215 -)
daughter of Lleiffer Mawr King of Colchester
Idwal Twrch Merrick (680 -)
son of Gwladys Ferch Lleiffer Mawr

Rhodvi Molwynog Merrick
son of Idwal Twrch Merrick
Conan Merrick Prince Of Wales (660 -)
son of Rhodvi Molwynog Merrick
Mervyn King of Gwynedd Merrick (750 - 844)
son of Conan Merrick Prince Of Wales
Rhodri Mawr (Rhoderick the Great) Merrick (810 - 878)
son of Mervyn King of Gwynedd Merrick
Llewelyn Merrick (1200 - 1280)
son of Rhodri Mawr (Rhoderick the Great) Merrick
Joan Daughter of King John I of Lackland (1197 - 1237)
wife of Llewelyn Merrick
John "Lackland" Plantagenet (Winmar) Winsor I (1167 - 1216)
father of Joan Daughter of King John I of Lackland
Eleanor Plantagenet (1215 - 1275)
daughter of John "Lackland" Plantagenet (Winmar) Winsor I
Eleanor De Montfort (1252 - 1282)
daughter of Eleanor Plantagenet
Ienen Ap Llewellyn (1460 -)
son of Eleanor De Montfort
John Ienen (1488 - 1523)
son of Ienen Ap Llewellyn
Ienen Ap John (1520 - 1554)
son of John Ienen
Janet Verch Ienen (1550 - 1589)
daughter of Ienen Ap John
John Merrick (1579 - 1650)
son of Janet Verch Ienen
William Merrick (1603 - 1689)
son of John Merrick
John Merrick (1656 - 1748)
son of William Merrick

John Merrick (1679 - 1778)
son of John Merrick
Isaac Merrick (1703 - 1787)
son of John Merrick
Israel Merrick (1733 - 1789)
son of Isaac Merrick
Israel Merrick (1766 - 1844)
son of Israel Merrick
Isaac Merrick (1791 - 1880)
son of Israel Merrick
Jacob B. Merrick (1825 - 1878)
son of Isaac Merrick
Daniel O. Merrick (1854 - 1930)
son of Jacob B. Merrick
Walter Truman Merrick (1895 - 1977)
son of Daniel O. Merrick
Robert W Merrick (1918 - 2000)
son of Walter Truman Merrick
Daniel Walter Merrick PhD
You are the son of Robert W Merrick

The *Desposyni*

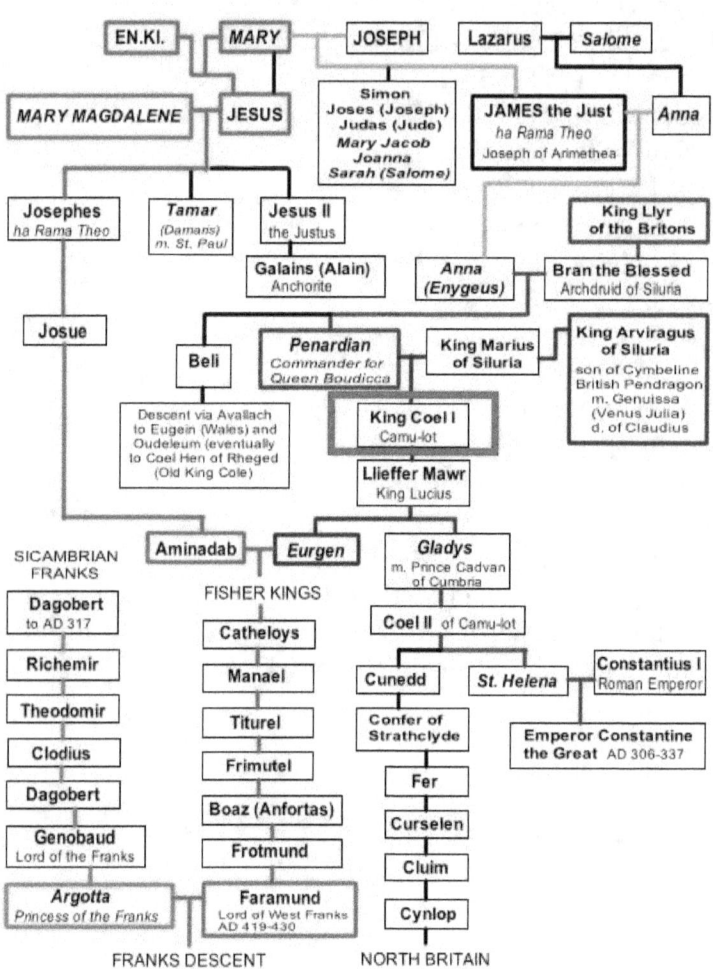

Source of Photo [19]

This chart shows the direct line through James the brother of Yahshua to King coel and the Mawr or Merrick line. Luke 3:23-38 Yahshua (Jesus) the son of Joseph, which

19 http://herebedragons.weebly.com/desposyni.html

was the son of Heli. Luke Also states that Elizabeth married to Zacharia the Priest of Levi was cousin of Mary. So Mary's mother was from the tribe of LEVI and and her father Heli was from the tribe of Judah. [Heli was the father of Marium (Mary) so in accord with the two shall be one, he was a son also.] 1st Cousin 49 Generations ago.

Heli father of Marium:
Which was the son of Matthat
which was the son of Levi,
which was the son of Melchi,
which was the son of Janna,
which was the son of Joseph,
Which was the son of Mattathias,
which was the son of Amos,
which was the son of Naum,
which was the son of Esli,
which was the son of Nagge,
Which was the son of Maath,
which was the son of Mattathias,
which was the son of Semei,
which was the son of Joseph,
which was the son of Juda,
Which was the son of Joanna,
which was the son of Rhesa,
which was the son of Zorobabel,
which was the son of Salathiel,
which was the son of Neri,
Which was the son of Melchi,
which was the son of Addi,
which was the son of Cosam,
which was the son of Elmodam,
which was the son of Er,
Which was the son of Jose,

which was the son of Eliezer,
which was the son of Jorim,
which was the son of Matthat,
which was the son of Levi,
Which was the son of Simeon,
which was the son of Juda,
which was the son of Joseph,
which was the son of Jonan,
which was the son of Eliakim,
Which was the son of Melea,
which was the son of Menan,
which was the son of Mattatha,
which was the son of Nathan,
which was the son of David, The King of Israe
Which was the son of Jesse,
which was the son of Obed,
which was the son of Booz,
which was the son of Salmon,
which was the son of Naasson,
Which was the son of Aminadab,
which was the son of Aram,
which was the son of Esrom,
which was the son of Phares,
which was the son of Judah, who with his borthers and
sister Dinah were the tribes of Israel who was also called
Jacob.
Which was the son of Jacob,
which was the son of Isaac,
which was the son of Abraham,
which was the son of Thara,
which was the son of Nachor,
Which was the son of Saruch,
which was the son of Ragau,
which was the son of Phalec,

which was the son of Heber,
which was the son of Sala,
Which was the son of Cainan,
which was the son of Arphaxad,
which was the son of Sem,
which was the son of Noah,
which was the son of Lamech,
Which was the son of Mathusala, who was the oldest man
in the world and on the day he died the flood came.
which was the son of Enoch,
which was the son of Jared,
which was the son of Maleleel,
which was the son of Cainan,
Which was the son of Enos,
which was the son of Seth,
which was the son of Adam,
which was the son of God, created the first man who had
Eve as his wife given him from Yahuah God, created from
him.

The Merrick Line

Adam
Seth
Enos
Cainan
Maleleel
Jared
Enoch
Mathusala
Lamech
Noah
Sem
Arphaxad

Cainan
Sala
Heber
Phalec
Ragau
Saruch
Nachor
Thara
Abraham
Isaac
Jacob who is also called Israel
Levi Son of Jacob who was called Isael
Merari
Mushi
Mahli
Libni
SHimel
Uzza
Shimea
Haggiah
Asaiah
Korah
Ebiasaph
Kore
SHallum
Uriyah
Rideyrn
Grad
Vrban
Triull
Deheweint
Tecvan
Merrick who was also called Murig (Also by way of

Coel)[20]
Mordaf
Seruan
Kedic
Dyfnwal Hen
Manogan
Beli Mawr (El Beli) who was married to the Prophetess
Anna daughter of Yoseph of Arimathea.
Ludd Llaw
Afallach
Owain
Prydein
Dubwn
Eufwn
Anwrid
Dufn
Doli
Cein
Tacitus
Pateruns
Aeternus
Cunedda Wledig King of North Wales
Einion Yrth
Cadwallon Lawhir (long Hand)
Maelgyn Gwynedd
Rhun Hir (The tall)
Hoel II
Beli
Lago
Cadvan Frist Prince of Wales
Cadwaladr (Last King of the United British Race)
Idwal Twrch

---

20 See Chart Page 64 of this book, by the brother of Yahshua James;
    Ibid

Rhodvi Molwynog

Conan the Great

Mervyn

Rohdri Mawr

Llewelyn The First (wife's line to the same Desposyni Kah'mari lineage)

Meredydd

Cydafael

Samuel

Madoc

Tydr

Torworth

David (as recorded in the records of George Byron Merrick and the British Archives)

Einion Sais

Heylin

Llewellyn (The Second, named for Lewite Tribe of Marari from historical genealogy) (1450 - 1485) is my 14th great grandfather

Merrick ap Llewelyn High Sheriff King Henry VIII Merrick (1480 - 1538) Variations in spelling Meyrick, Myrick, Mirrick, M620 Codex of names Soundex system of Phonetic Genealogy. (Also Murig ap Liewellyn first Surnamed for the tribe of Merari by King Henry the VII) son of Lewellyn Merrick

Sir Rev John Merrick (1513 - 1595) Who with his brother Roland D Merrick DD translated the Bible into Welsh and worked on the foundations of the King James version of the Bible in English. son of Merrick ap Llewelyn High Sheriff King Henry VIII Merrick

Rev William Merrick (1546 - 1589) son of Sir Rev John Merrick

John Merrick (1579 - 1650) son of Rev William Merrick - Through His Mother Janet came the line of Matthat of

Judah, Grandfather of Yahshua Messiah who is called Christ.
William Merrick (1603 - 1689) son of John Merrick
John Merrick (1656 - 1748) son of William Merrick
John Merrick (1679 - 1778) son of John Merrick
Isaac Merrick (1703 - 1787) son of John Merrick Who fought in the Revolutionary War
Israel Merrick (1733 - 1789) son of Isaac Merrick Who was the first McKean county Clerk Assistant and the First Baptist School teacher in Smethport PA.
Israel Merrick (1766 - 1844) son of Israel Merrick Who came to Pennsylvania in 1804
Isaac Merrick (1791 - 1880) son of Israel Merrick
Dr. Jacob B. Merrick (1825 - 1878) son of Isaac Merrick.
Dr. Daniel O. Merrick DDS (1854 - 1930) son of Jacob B. Merrick. Who's wife is from the line of Pracila Mullens who came on the Mayflower.
Walter Truman Merrick (1895 - 1977) son of Daniel O. Merrick
Robert W Merrick (1918 - 2000) son of Walter Truman Merrick
Daniel Walter Merrick PhD - You are the son of Robert W Merrick
Jeremiah L Merrick My Son 107th in the line from Adam.

Desposyni (Greek δεσπόσυνοι, desposynoi, "those of the master") is a term used uniquely by Sextus Julius Africanus[35] to refer to the relatives of Jesus.
The Gospels mention four brothers of Jesus—James, Joses, Simon, and Jude[94]—along with two sisters, named by Epiphanius[95] as Mary and Salome (or Anna and Salome).[96] pronounced: "Des Poah S' nee"
https://en.wikipedia.org/wiki/Genealogy_of_Jesus

Kahmari: Term used to denote the close relatives of the blood lines of those associated family members of the levitical lines of the mother of Mary from the tribe of Levi.

Kah is a chaldean word for Spirit, Mari is the line of worship leaders of Levi that played music from the scriptures in

1Ch_6:47 The son of Mahli, the son of Mushi, the son of Merari, the son of Levi. 1Ch 23:5 Moreover four thousand were porters; and four thousand praised the LORD with the instruments which I made, said David, to praise therewith.

1Ch 23:6 And David divided them into courses among the sons of Levi, namely, Gershon, Kohath, and Merari.

2Ch_34:12 And the men did the work faithfully: and the overseers of them were Jahath and Obadiah, the Levites, of the sons of Merari; and Zechariah and Meshullam, of the sons of the Kohathites, to set it forward; and other of the Levites, all that could skill of instruments of musick.

The Family name Merrick came from the mixture in Europe of Merari and Musickah from the area of Ukraine after the dispersion fouund in Ezra in the bible. The sons had married gentile women and were put out of the Assyraian return and moved north into what is now Afghanistan and Ukraine about 700BC. The words for Music in Russian and Ukrainian language was Musickah denoting the Kah of the Spirit and the use of music in worship. The combination of the words for the tribe of

Levi which was Merari the son of Levi became Mer-ic-kah for the Merarites who played Music. The Merari were not son's of Aaron, so they did not have the title of Cohanim Gadol or High Priest but being of Levi had the duties of carrying the outer temple poles, curtains, and other parts of the tent which made up the temple. They also played the worship music and carried the instruments for worship. When King Henry the 7th first made surnames for those of the British Isles they also knew of those who were from Royal lines from David and the tribes of Merari and Levi, and thus appropriately named the sons of the lines by the fathers before them.

The original word for the tribe of Levi in ancient Hebrew was in fact Lewite (Leu White) which is the phonetic root of the word for Louie and Llewellyn the king by that name in Wales.

The phonetic soundex system was created for genealogists to group surnames into simalar sounding names coming from a same common ancestor. For Merrick the Codex #M620 (Jewish Gen Code-M code 695000 or 694500) is used to identify the lines that came from the earliest known ancestor as in Wales as Merrick son of Llewellyn who was also called Murig. The associated line of Mawr, Mar, Merari, and Mir with phonetic Mer and Zimmer or Zimmar taken also from the instrument of the same name believed to have been a type of harp in ancient times. In Germanic form the ZA or THE and MAR for Merarite. From these progressions of the name came the word Singer also.

In America the house of John Merrick of the Virginia Company of London held indentured servants in exchange for passage to the new world. For seven years half of all the crops and earnings came to the company in payment for freedom.

As a result of this begrudging over this contract after the fact, it became common slang to call the country "A Merrick A" because of owing half of all to the Merrick family company. The Italian Roman Catholic Church claimed that the man name Amerigo had first claimed to discover this new world and that it was the reason for this name. Later the fruad was discovered that Amerigo had not traveled to the new world yet the Roman Catholic Author's of books seemed to continue to rewrite history in favor of this liar as the one who discovered America. Yet the Merrick Indians were also among the first contacts after 1492 when Columbus came to the new world and they held that phonetic name for over one thousand years. The recent studies in DNA have shown that the Merrick Native American tribes along with the Seneca and Cherokee have roots in the Hebrew Tribal lineage. Artifacts found in the burial mounds of Ohio have been proven to have the sacred name of God in Hebrew, the letters Y-H-U-H on them and the Cherokee word for the Great Spirit is "Hey Yah Who Way AH" similar in sound to Yahuah and Yahweh. DNA matching has proven that the Egyptian and Hebrew lines are mixed into the native American tribes. This was discovered when Dr Davies of Oxford found that Nicotine and Coca were in all the mummies and the chemical compounds were used in ancient embalming. The pattern of Evidence shows that the Hebrews in slavery in Egypt, came in ships to the Americas to gather tobacco and Coca leaves which were used in the mummification process. No doubt, now by DNA proven, some ships did not survive the journey and the stranded people became cultivators of plants and remained in the Americas finding freedom there before the time of Christ. The resulting inner-marriage of the Amer-Asians became what are known as native American tribes. When one looks at the Egyptian and Hebrew influences found in burial practice and pyramid like tombs along with the ancient Hebrew words for the name of God, this fact can not be disputed.

I have no doubt that this country was name for the Merari Hebrew who first came here and named it such. Along with the folklore of the Merrick Virginia Company being in disdain for it's part in slavery for passage, the resulting mockery of "A Merrick Ah" became a type of phonetic history repeating itself.

*This is taken from Mostyn MS. 117 which dates from the late thirteenth century and may be by the same scribe who wrote Llyfr Taliesin. It may have been based on material from the twelfth century but with the first genealogy extended to Llywelyn ap Gruffudd. The names that were omitted from MS. 117 were filled in through phonetic macthing and cross reference to Bible scriptures.

**The line of : m. Endos m. Endolen m. 49-Aflach m. Flech m. 48-Llud m. 47-Beli mawr m. 46-Manogan m. 45-Dyfynwal hen m.
Shown as wife on other manuscript:Gorwynyawn m. Kamber m. Brutus m. Siluius m.
Ascanius m. Eneas m. Anchises m. Capis m. Assaraccus m. Trois m.[Eri}coinus m. Dardan m.
(Number of generations show other decent from DODANIM from japath Gen. 10:4)
Iubiter m. 17-Saru[rn] m. 13-Celi m. Creti m. Cipri m. Cetim m. Ienan m.=Javan Gen.10

from Japath=Iaphed m. Noe hen m. Lamech m.
[M]a[th]usalem m. Enoc m. Iareth
m. Malalel m. Kainan m. Enos m. Seth m. Adam m. Duw.
Note that compared to Bible
Records some names are missing. This line shown through
Yuri (Uri) [Eri] to Saru and
to Japath through the line of Magnus Maximus Roman
decent. (Which line also claimed
to be from Judah by way of Joseph of Arimathea). In
MS117 Coel Codebog listed out of order
and clear decent had to of been through Prince Meuric or
Manogan.
Conflicting lines= Shem>Levi>Uri>Coel
Codebog>Merrick; Japath>Dardan (Dodanim)>Saru
(which was a line of shem)>manogan>Coel
Codebog>Merrick; Judah>Joesph of Arimathea>
Magnus Maximus>Mawr>Coel Codebog>Merrick

***Bonhed Gwyr y Gogledd (the Descent of the Men of
the North) is found in a number of manuscripts, the
earliest being Peniarth MS.45 of the second half of
the thirteenth century. It overlaps with both the Harleian
MS. 3859 (1100 though the genealogies were probably
compiled before 988) and the Jesus College MS.20
(late fourteenth century but probably compiled in the
thirteenth century)

****Records researched by M.L.B. Merrick and Society
of the Cincinnati of Maryland; Robert Graft Merrick,
family Historian; England © Jan.5 , 1974.

My Merrick lines are from Mostyn MS. 117 which dates
from the late thirteenth century. The earliest being

Peniarth MS.45 of the second half of the thirteenth century. It overlaps with both the Harleian MS. 3859 and the Jesus College MS.20 (998-1400)

Now during the period of the Safrahime, 400BC to 70AD, many bought genealogy to claim kinship to Abraham. So are we really Jews as the manuscripts suggest? Did we come from Merari? (Num.26:57) Get Merrick History Books by Dr Dan at www.YahBible.com

Previous (OLD) Version of the line which is corrected above:

MALE MERRICK, Codex #M620 (Jewish Gen Code-M code 695000 or 694500)Genealogy: Male Merrick Lineage from : Yah, GOD: To be praised, honored, and glorified forever Creator of the first man- As Recorded in First Chronicles 1:1 ; 1:24-28:
1-ADAM +Eve ~4000 BC,
2-Seth ,
3-Enoch ,
4-Kenan ,
5-MahalaleYah ,
6-Jered ,
7-Henoch (Enoch) ,
8-Methuselah , (oldest man died at 800+)
9-Lamech ,
10-Noah ~2000 BC ,
11-Shem ,
12-Arphaxad ,
13-Shelah ,
14-Eber ,

15-Peleg ,

16-Reu ,

17-Serug ,

18-Nahor ,

19-Terah ,

20-Abraham , + Sarah

21-Isaac ,

22-Jacob who's name was changed to ISRIYAH (Israel) ,

23-Levi ,

24-Merari (Numbers 26:57) B.C. 1452 , (first Phonetic root)

25-Mushi ,

26-Mahli ,

27-Libni ,

28-Shimei ,

29-Uzza ,

30-Shimea ,

31-Haggiah ,

32-Asaiah (I Chron. 6:29-32) "And these are those who David set over the service of song in the house of YAH veh after that the ark had rest.

And they ministered before the dwelling place of the tabernacle of the congregation with singing." ,

33-Korah ,

34-Ebiasaph ,

35-Kore ,

36-Shallum 536 BC ,

37-Uri-yah, (Ezra 10:24 -*Welsh=Keyeirn m. M for Merari also MAWR-Eng.& Ukraine=the Yuri Mer ic Ka; Merarites under King EURI (yuri)
moved through Babylon to Ukraine region and the Caccus Mountains through Germanus to England and Wales),

38-Rideyrn m.,

39-Grad m.,

40-Vrba(n) m.,
41-Triuil m.,
42-Deheweint m.,
43-Tecvan m.,
44-King Cole Codebog of the Merari (Welsh Keneu Coel godebawc m. ~262 B.C. FIRST KING OF BRITON - The British (Covanant) Race.
Who's sons succeeded until- (as recorded in Burke's Genealogy Records ~15 generations to King Henery III, King Edward I &II through Brothers to the Merrick line) * [47-Beli m. 65-Run m. 64-Maelgwn Gwyned, herwyd dull y beird. Namyn o herwyd yr Istoria Beli oed vab 62-Eynyan vab 64-Maelgwn, y
gwr a uu petweryd brenhin
ar Ynys Prydein gwedy Arthur. The line of 64-Maelgwn Gwynedd spouse to King Arthur through the brother of El Mar. 64-Maelgwn oed vab 63-Katwallawn llawhir m. 62-Eynyawn yrth m. 61-Kuneda wledic m. 60-Edern m. 59-Padern peisrud. (m.)/from coel codebog//] The line of 61-Cunedda Wledig
through: (60&59)
45-Mordaf m. (MAR)***
46-Seruan m. ***
47-Kedic m.***
48-Dyfynwal Hen m. (Daniel) Abt.150bc + **&***
49-Manogan m.
50-El (Beli) Mawr (the Great), King of Britain, Abt 110 bc - + Don ferch Mathonwy
51-Lludd Llaw Ereint (the Silver-Handed), King of Britain, Abt 80 bc -
52-Afallach ap Lludd, Abt 45 bc -
53-Owain ap Afallach, Abt 10 bc -
54-Prydein ap Owain, Abt 25 -
55-Dubwn ap Prydein, Abt 60 -

56-Eufwn ap Dubwn, Abt 95 -
57-Anwrid ap Eufwn, Abt 130 -
58-(Gwr-)Dufn ap Anwrid, Abt 165 -
59-(Gwr-)Doli ap Dufn, Abt 200 -
60-(Gwr-)Cein ap Doli, Abt 235 -
61-Tacitus ap Cein, Abt 270 -
62-Paternus Pasrut (of the Red Robe), Abt 305 -
63-Aeternus ap Padeyrn, Abt 340 -
64-Cunedda Wledig (the Imperator), King of North Wales,
+ Gwawl ferch Coel, Abt 384
65-Einion Yrth (the Impetuous), King of Gwynedd, Abt
419 -...+Prawst ferch Deithlyn, Abt 420
66-Cadwallon Lawhir (Long Hand), King of Gwynedd,
Abt 450 - 517..+Meddyf ferch Maeldaf,abt460
67-Maelgwn Gwynedd alias Hir (the Tall), King of
Gwynedd, Abt 480 - 549.......+Gwallwen ferch Afallach,
Abt 490 -**
68-Rhun Hir (the Tall), King of Gwynedd, Abt 508 -
586.......+Perfawr ferch Rhun, Abt 510
(also known as Urien, Lord of Rhegid, 590 AD)
69-Rimo ferch Rhun, Abt 528 -.....+Hoel II Fychan (the
Small), Abt 522 - 547
70- El (Beli) ap Rhun, King of Gwynedd, Abt 530 -
599.......+Unknown
71-Iago ap Beli, King of Gwynedd, Abt 560 -
613.........+Unknown
72-Cadvan First Prince of Wales & King of North Wales
(Catamanus) Cadfan ap Iago, King of Gwynedd, Abt 580 -
625...............+Afandreg Ddu (the Black), Abt 584 -
73-King Cadwaladr 650 A.D. Last Crowned King of the
British Race.Cadwallon ap Cadfan, King of Gwynedd,
Abt 600 - 634
74-Idwal Twrch, Abt 680
75-Rhodvi Molwynog 703 A.D.

76-Conan 720 A.D.

77-Mervyn Vrych (Merfyn Frych -kings of Gwynedd =
Nest /kings of Powys)

78-Rhodri Mawr (Rhoderick the Great) 843 A.D.

79-Llewelyn (Excluded from his crown by his uncle
Cadell.) married Angharad Queen of Powys, daughter of
Owen ap Howel ap Cadell ap 78 Rhodri Mawr

79-Meredydd Meredith King of Powys, slain 998AD(ap
Owen because he was his Cousins son
by Biblical Law [Meredydd {ap Llewelyn Biological
Father}ap Owen ap howel Dha the good
King of south Wales, ap Cadell ap 78 Rhodri Mawr)

80-Cydafael Ynnyd (Lord of Cydewain, Montgomery
County, Judge of Powys+Arienwen ap Jarwarth

81-Samuel

82-Madoc

83-Tydr +Nest ferch Tudor

84-Torworth +Agnes ferch Robin

85-Davydd +Janet ferch David

86-Einion Sais (saxon fought in the wars of King Henry
V)

87-Heylin

88-LLewellyn +Angharad ap William

89-Meyrick/Meuric April 25, 1509 Captian of the Guard
to King Henry VII and High Sheriff of
Anglesey County - Surnamed Merrick by King Henry the
VIII as from Merari and Meurick for
"Guardian" (As in Guardians of the Arc). +Margaret ap
Roland

90-Rt. Rev. Roland Merrick D.D. Bishop of Bangor,
Anglesey, Wales born 1505 +Catherine Burill

91-John Merrick Member of the Virginia Company of
London by charter granted by the King
on May 23, 1609. +Lucy Powell

81

92-Henry Merrick +?
93-John Merrick + Elizabeth?, Who came to America in 1663 to Barbados and later Va. USA.
94-Daniel Merrick 1645 +? First permanent settler in Talbot County Maryland keeping the
" HOUSE OF JOHN MERRICK, MERCHANTS" of the VIRGINIA COMPANY OF LONDON.
(F.H. Merrick shows here: Julian Merrick 1626-1718)
**** First came to Barbados and came to the
New World in 1663, Settled in MD 1669.)
95-John Merrick 1669 +Jane Walker
96-Isacc Merrick 1703 +Rachel Skinner
97-Israel Merrick 1733 +Mary Lane
98-Israel Merrick 1766 ,(Tioga, Pa. 1801-04) +Mary Lockwood Brockway
99-Isaac Merrick 1791 +Polly Vanatter +Clara ?
100-Dr. Jacob B. Merrick 1826 +Lucy A. Burns
101-Dr. Daniel O. Merrick +Pearl Vail
102-Pastor Walter T. Merrick +Edna Pearl Redfield
103-Robert W. Merrick 1918 - 2000 +Laura M. Sloan 1925 - 1998
104-Cpt. Daniel W. Merrick 1958 +Olga Gorobets (Immagrant Ukraine)
105-Jeremiyah L. Merrick Siblings: Yuri, Igor, Tannyah, Victoria, Danitra, Julia.
106-Karina 2005 (Julia + Roman)

References:

http://en.wikipedia.org/wiki/Second_Temple_Judaism

Throughout the history of Israel, high priests were chosen by lot from among the Levites. ...
The position was subsequently bought with bribes from

wealthy Sadducean families,
who agreed ... This family was extremely wealthy and
corrupt, functioning much like a "mafia. ....
1 Flavius Josephus " The Wars of the Jews " IV, 3.7.
Also Josephus give account that the high priesthood was
appointed by Ceasers to Romans during this period.

http://en.wikipedia.org/wiki/Merari

http://en.wikipedia.org/wiki/Merarites

Merarite Clan
The Merarites were given twelve cities from the tribes of
Zebulun, Reuben, and Gad. Their city allotment can be
found in Joshua 21:34-40.
From the tribe of Zebulun
Jokneam, Kartah, Kimnah, Nahalal
From the tribe of Reuben
Bezer, Jahaz, Kedemoth, Mephaath
From the tribe of Gad
Ramoth-Gilead, a city of refuge, Mahanaim, Heshbon,
Jazer
In all, the tribe of Levi received a total of forty-eight
towns in the "territory held by the Israelites".
Only 9 rested south of Jerusalem. The heartland of Israel,
Judah, Ephraim, and Manasseh, did not receive the
majority of
Levitical cities. Rather, most cities lie in the peripheral
areas to the north and east of the heartland.
Much of the area encompassed by these cities of the tribe
of Levi lie within Canaanite controlled territory until the
time of
David. Indeed, God's presence was needed most in these
areas under idolatrous influence.

Not only did the tribe of Levi receive these cities, but Scripture indicates they also received the pasture lands surrounding each town as well.

Numbers 35 records an interesting conversation between God and Moses. God instructs Moses on how each city given to t

he tribe of Levi is to be structured. God's attention to detail is incredible.

Each Levite town has pasture lands for "their cattle, flocks and all their other livestock".

The pasture lands around each town are to extend fifteen hundred feet from the town wall. Three thousand feet are allotted

for each pastureland, on each side of the city: 3,000 ft. on the east side; 3,000 ft. on the south side; 3,000 ft. on the west side; and 3,000 ft. on the north side.

The town itself was to rest in the center, surrounded on each side by huge pastures. The Levites were to be self-sufficient, relying solely on God for sustenance.

God, in turn, provided each city with enough cattle, flocks, livestock, land, and crops to be self-reliant.

Each of the tribes of Israel, in essence, paid a tithe to God; in the form of towns and land, within their respective tribal allotment.

These were to be given specifically to the tribe of Levi.

Published in 1847 by John Wright Printer, The History of the Tribe of Levi Considered
is an in-depth study in into the tribe of Levi. Click on the link below to re-direct to Amazon.com.

The History Of The Tribe Of Levi Considered (1847)

Mostyn MS. 117
http://en.wikipedia.org/wiki/King_Arthur's_family

Bibliography

Bromwich, R. Trioedd Ynys Prydein: the Welsh Triads
(Cardiff: University of Wales, 1978)

Bromwich, R. and Simon Evans, D. Culhwch and Olwen.
An Edition and Study of the Oldest Arthurian Tale
(Cardiff: University of Wales Press, 1992)

Bryant, N. The High Book of the Grail: A translation of
the thirteenth century romance of Perlesvaus (Brewer,
1996)

Coe, J. B. and Young, S. The Celtic Sources for the
Arthurian Legend (Llanerch, 1995).

Green, T. "The Historicity and Historicisation of Arthur",
Arthurian Resources, retrieved on 22-06-2007

Green, T. "Tom Thumb and Jack the Giant Killer: Two
Arthurian Fairytales?" in Folklore 118.2 (August, 2007),
pp.123-40

Green, T. Concepts of Arthur (Stroud: Tempus, 2007)
ISBN 978-0-7524-4461-1 [1]

Higham, N. J. King Arthur, Myth-Making and History
(London: Routledge, 2002).

Jones, T. and Jones, G. The Mabinogion (London: Dent,
1949)

Kibler, W. and Carroll, C. W. Arthurian Romances
(Harmondsworth, Penguin, 1991)

Lacy, N. J. Lancelot-Grail: The Old French Arthurian
Vulgate and Post-Vulgate in Translation (New York:
Garland, 1992-6), 5 vols

Padel, O. J. Arthur in Medieval Welsh Literature (Cardiff:
University of Wales Press, 2000) ISBN 978-0-7524-4461-
1

Roberts, B. F. "Geoffrey of Monmouth, Historia Regum
Britanniae and Brut Y Brenhinedd" in R. Bromwich,

A.O.H. Jarman and B.F. Roberts (edd.) The Arthur of the Welsh (Cardiff: University of Wales Press, 1991), pp.98-116

Rowland, J. Early Welsh Saga Poetry: a Study and Edition of the Englynion (Cambridge, 1990)

Sims-Williams, P. "The Early Welsh Arthurian Poems" in R. Bromwich, A.O.H. Jarman and B.F. Roberts (edd.) The Arthur of the Welsh (Cardiff: University of Wales Press, 1991), pp.33-71

Peniarth MS.45
http://en.wikipedia.org/wiki/Bonedd_Gwŷr_y_Gogledd
Koch, John T. "Cynwydion." In Celtic Culture. A Historical Encyclopedia, ed. John T. Koch. 5 vols. Santa Barbara et al., 2006. pp. 541–2.

Editions and translations

Bromwich, Rachel (ed.). Trioedd Ynys Prydein. The Triads of the Island of Britain. Cardiff: University of Wales Press, 1978; revised ed. 1991. pp. 238–9 (Appendix II)

Matthews, Keith (ed.). Bonedd Gwyr y Gogledd. 2000. Online edition (not peer-reviewed).

Jackson, Kenneth H. Language and History in Early Britain. Edinburgh University Press, 1953.

Bartrum, Peter C. Early Welsh genealogical tracts. Cardiff, 1966.

Rachel Bromwich and R. Brinley Jones (eds.), Astudiaethau ar yr Hengerdd. Cardiff, 1978.

http://www.tristanandisolde.net/articles/article/welsh-triads/peniarth-ms-45/triad-23-english-translation

Harleian MS. 3859

http://en.wikipedia.org/wiki/Harleian_genealogies

http://www.maryjones.us/ctexts/genealogies.html

Jesus College MS.20

http://en.wikipedia.org/wiki/Genealogies_from_Jesus_Col
lege_MS_20

http://www.maryjones.us/ctexts/jesus20gen.html

The National Library of Wales, Aberystwyth
http://ldolphin.org/cooper/appen4.html

1. Dingestow Court Manuscript - early 13th cent.

2. Peniarth MS. 44 = Hen. 315 (prey. 21) - early 13th cent.

3. Peniarth MS. 45 = Hen. 536 (prey. 29) - late 13th cent.

4. Peniarth MS. 46 = Hen. 27 - early 14th cent.

5. Peniarth MS. 21 Hen. 50 (prey. 16) - early 14th cent.

6. Peniarth MS. 19 = Hen. 15 - c. 1400.

7. Peniarth MS. 22 = Hen. 318 - 1444.

8. Pemarth MS. 24 = Hen. 175 - 1477.

9. Peniarth MS. 23 = Hen. 313 - mid. 15th cent.

10. Peniarth MS. 25 = Hen. 305 - c. 1500.

11. Peniarth MS. 212 Hen. 319 - c. 1565.

12. Peniarth MS. 168 Hen. 437 - 1589-90.

13. Peniarth MS. 118 = Hen. 518 - late 16th cent.

14. Peniarth MS. 261 = Hen. 446 - 16th cent.

15. Peniarth MS. 260 = Hen. 442 - 16th cent.

16. Peniarth MS. 162 = Hen. 354 - late 16th cent.

17. Peniarth MS. 266 = Hen. 55 (prey. 3) - 1634.

18. Peniarth MS. 314 = Hen. 293 (prey. 87 and 21) - 1634-1641.

19. Peniarth MS. 264 = Hen. 272 (prey. 2, 55 and LX) -1635 - 6.

20. Peniarth MS. 265 = Hen. 439 (prey. i, 72 and LIV) -1641.

21. Peniarth MS. 270 = Hen. 530 -

22. Llanstephan MS. 1 = Shirburn Castle MS. 113 C. 18 -early 13th cent.

23. Llanstephan MS. S = Shirburn Castle MS. 34 - early 14th cent.

24. Llanstephan MS. 188 - mid. 16th cent.

25. Llanstephan MS. 195 - c. 1570.

26. Llanstephan MS. 59 = Shirburn Castle C. 7 - late 16th cent.

27. LianstePhan MS. 129 = Shirburu Castle D. 17 - early 17th cent.

28. Llanstephan MS. 137 = Shirburn Castle D. 12 - c. 1640.

29. Llanstephan MS. 149 = Shirburn Castle D. 15. - c. 1700

30. Mostyn MS. 117 - late 13th cent.

31. Mostyn MS. 116 - early 14th cent.

32. Mostyn MS. 109 - 16th cent.

33. Mostyn MS. 159 - 1586-7.

34. Mostyn MS. 115 - 17th cent.

35. Mostyn MS. 211 - c. 1685.

36. Panton MS. 9 - c. 1760.

37. Panton MS. 68 - 18th cent.

38. The Book of Basingwerk MS. (alias The Black Book of Basingwerk Abbey) - 14th and 15th cents.

39. Additional MS. 13 - B = Williams MS. 216 - early 17th cent.

40. Additional MS. 11 - D Williams MS. 213 - 1694.

41. Additional MS. 312 Williams MS. 514 - early 18th cent.

42. Additional MS. 23 - B Williams MS. 227 - c. 1775.

Free Public Library, Cardiff, Wales

43. Cardiff (Havod) MS. 1 - early 14th cent.

44. Cardiff (Havod) MS. 2 - 15th cent 'or earlier'.

45. Cardiff (Havod) MS. 21 - 1641.

46. Cardiff MS. 21 = Phillipps 13720, part III - 1569.

47. Cardiff MS. 61 = (Tonn 21) - 1734.

48. Cardiff MS. 62 = (Tonn 22) - 1754.

Jesus College Library, Oxford

49. MS. CXI = 1, Hist. MSS. Coin., Report of MSS in the Welsh Lang - c. 1380.

50. MS. CXLI = 6, Hist. MSS. Corn., Report of MSS in the Welsh Lang - c. 1471.

51. MS. LXI = 8, Hist. MSS. Coin., Report of MSS in the Welsh Lang (aka the Tysilio Chronicle) - late 15th cent.

52. MS. XXVIII = 19 Hist. MSS. Coin. - 1695.

British Museum, London

53. Additional MS. 19,709 = MS. 14, Hist. MSS. Corn. -early 14th cent.

54. Cotton, Cleopatra B. V., = MS. 15, Hist. MSS. Corn. -14th cent.

55. Additional MS. 14,903 = MS. 17, Hist. MSS. Corn. - early 16th cent.

56. Additional MS. 15,566 = MS. 16, Hist. MSS. Corn. - late 16th cent.

57. Additional MS. 14,872 = MS. 41, Hist. MSS. Corn. - post 1632.

58. Additional MS. 15,003 - 18th cent.

USA References to Merrick Jewish and Non Jewish in practice :

The Genealogy of Merrick, Mirick, Mtrick Family 1902, George Byron Merrick, Tracy Gibbs Company Publishers C 1902

The Story of Myricks, Allie Goodwin Myrick Bowden, The J W Burke Company 1952

Merrick's of Talbout County Maryland, M. L. Bushey Merrick, 1978

Merrick Genealogy, R. Ladd English, 1960 to 1995 Records

The History and Genealogy of Merrick, 1902; 1995 Higgdonson

The Merrick Family History, D W Merrick, 2nd Edition, 2012, Eternal light & Power Co. Publishing.

AMerrickA
4981876
ISBN-13: 978-1501050527
ISBN-10: 1501050524 NSSAR Library
BISAC: Reference / Genealogy / History
Ancestors Of Daniel W Merrick PhD
4416967 ISBN-13: 978-1492253549
ISBN-10: 1492253545 NSSAR Library
BISAC: Reference / Genealogy
Goy Vey! I'm Jewish?
3963482
ISBN-13: 978-1479107940
ISBN-10: 1479107948 NSSAR Library
BISAC: Social Science / Jewish Studies
Merrick (Family history and Genealogy)
3908513 ISBN-13: 978-1477659380
ISBN-10: 1477659382 NSSAR Library
BISAC: Reference / Genealogy
The Royal Ancestors of Merrick
4975335 ISBN-13: 978-1501002687
ISBN-10: 1501002686 NSSAR Library
BISAC: Reference / Genealogy
Two Daniels
4272892 ISBN-13: 978-1484900284

ISBN-10: 1484900286 NSSAR Library
BISAC: Reference / Genealogy
Merrick Foundation Org
"The R1b Claim and Merari - Cohanim Genealogy"
FTDNA Com
http://www.familytreedna.com/public/Merrick

The above list of chronicles that give the history of the
early Britons, constitutes a rather large percentage
of the total number of Welsh manuscripts that have come
down to us from medieval times. Given that they
are all cataloged in easily accessible collections, it is
astonishing that even their very existence goes
unmentioned by most scholars who are aware of them, and
that British history prior to 55 BC remains a
blank page. But perhaps their acknowledgment would lead
the recorded history of the early Britons
uncomfortably back to Genesis, and that is a concept that
modernism simply could not accommodate.
So when we talk of this Biblical connection it is a clear
one, from the text found known as the Dead Sea
Scrolls also, to 262BC these records have survived. The
date of the copies has little effect on the age
of the genealogies, and a long standing record to which
this Merrick, Merari, Llewelyn, Levi, and Jacob
and the tribes of Israel have been recorded. The CO EL
and CO HEN ties are beyond dispute in my opinion.

Related Audio Productions:
http://rdjcatalog.com/podariffic/2015/10/16/faith-radio-
melech-tzadic-cohanim-shalom/
Faith Radio – Bennett Greenspan Family Tree DNA
http://rdjcatalog.com/podariffic/2013/03/08/faith-radio-
bennett-greenspan-family-tree-dna/

Dan also had an appearance in the PBS film "Smethport Our Home Town." talking about local pioneer history and genealogy:

https://www.youtube.com/watch?
v=jvs9RQIMSPc#action=share

© 2015 MerrickFoundation.Org; Eternal Light & Power Company Publishing; Est. 1992; D.W. Merrick PhD. First Published May 24, 1998-Feb.12, 1999 Daniel Merrick © 1997-2015 Merrick Foundation.Org

Conclusion

It is important to note that there are now absolute DNA evidences or proofs of direct lines from any biological children of Messiah Yahshua. To spite many books and movies claiming a blood line of Christ, the evidence is that there are only cousins and now ancient manuscript of genealogy has ever been found that proved any modern claim of the Priory of Zion by direct children.

Yet the lines we have found with ancient manuscripts show many lines from those who were directly related to Messiah who is called Christ, but only cousins from uncles and aunts and by brothers and sisters of Messiah as we find these also listed in the Bible.

As a 1st cousin of Messiah with both Merarite Levi DNA with proven J1b and R1b lines by ancient documentation, I find it interesting that this lineage was only revealed to public view over the last few short decades.

At one time such were sought by the church of Rome and others for extermination as found record of such from history. It is seen in my own family tree that there seems to be a mantle of the Holy Spirit or Roauch Ha Kodesh in the line where many were called to service of Messiah in Faith and work in ministry and work to translate the Bible and the Gospel in published form for the world to know Him who is Yahshua Messiah. As more lines are called today back home to Israel in discovery of their Jewish DNA, I can only be amazed that this history was preserved by the hand of Yahuah God to give me such a heritage of FAITH in this knowledge of who I am. Yahshua had Judah, David, Levi, Merari, and Aaron in his DNA through his mother Marium as the prophets foretold. Melech Cohanim Gadol Zadic Shalom Yahshua Messiah The King and High Priest of Righteousness and Peace is Yahshua Messiah. His lineage are being gathered to return to Israel for His coming again as the scriptures say would happen in these last days. [21]

---

21 http://www.thenazareneway.com/desposyni.htm ;
https://www.geni.com/surnames/desposyni ;
http://herebedragons.weebly.com/desposyni.html

ISBN-13: 978-1518796913

ISBN-10: 1518796915

For More books on Genealogical Studies on the
Merrick line of Royal and Hebrew descendants visit

MerrickFoundation.Org

and

YahBible.Com

© 2015 Eternal Light & Power Company Publishing
Daniel W Merrick PhD; CYMG, Smethport, Pa. 16749
www.YahBible.com

www.ingramcontent.com/pod-product-compliance
Lightning Source LLC
Chambersburg PA
CBHW071215280526
45787CB00002B/696